The
Working
Parents'
Handbook

How to Succeed at Work,
Raise Your Kids,
Maintain a Home,
and Still Have Time for You

Katherine Murray

Park Avenue

An imprint of JIST Works, Inc.

The Working Parents' Handbook
How to Succeed at Work, Raise Your Kids, Maintain a Home, and Still Have Time for You
Copyright © 1996 by Katherine Murray

Published by **Park Avenue Productions**
An imprint of JIST Works, Inc.
720 N. Park Avenue
Indianapolis, IN 46202-3431
Phone: 317-264-3720   Fax: 317-264-3709
E-mail: JISTWorks@AOL.com
See back page of this book for other books of interest.

Interior Illustrations by Bruce Berrigan

Printed in the United States of America

99 98 97   5 4 3 2

Library of Congress Cataloging-in-Publication Data

ISBN: 1-57112-075-0

To all working parents,
everywhere

Acknowledgments

The process of writing a book is not unlike raising a child. (Except it's a lot quicker and a lot less expensive!) It requires the help, insight, and direction of a number of talented people. I'd like to thank all these special people who have made writing and publishing *The Working Parents' Handbook* a wonderful experience:

James Irizarry, publisher, for believing in the project from the start and seeing it through to a finished book.

Connie Horner, my dear friend, research assistant, and biggest source of encouragement. Without you, Connie, much of the research for this book would never have been done.

Dr. Ted Sharpe, who reviewed and made suggestions for the chapters dealing with emotional issues. Thank you for providing your expertise—it has greatly added to the book.

Sherri Emmons, editor extraordinaire, who made invaluable suggestions and improvements throughout the development and editing stages of this book. Thanks, Sherri.

Wendy Prescott, for the wonderful, inviting, and useable design. Her careful design and layout of all the many elements makes this a book readers will enjoy spending time with.

And most of all, to my children, Kelly, Christopher, and Cameron, who make my life more wonderful, more joyful, and more challenging than I ever dreamed possible. They have provided—unwittingly and, in some cases, unwillingly—many of the examples for this book. Whether I am in work mode (glasses on, at the computer) or in Mom mode (playing "Donkey Kong Country" or, yes, baking cookies), they are at the center of my heart. I am truly blessed to be their mother.

v

Thanks, Mom and Dad!

Many thanks to these mothers and fathers who contributed their real-life stories and experiences to make *The Working Parents' Handbook* a better book:

Louis Ater	Pat Jones
Bill Alfee	Toni Lee
Wendy Alfee	Lisa Levins
Victoria Baker	Karen Livisee
Donneal R. Cottrill	Carol Mauer
Pam Eakins	Peggy Norris
Patti Fleming	Staci Rich
Janet Gagneur	John Smith
Duane Hampton	Debra Spencer
Peggy Payne Hood	Kathy Strickland
Melinda Hornback	Dan Turner
Connie Horner	Reva Turner
April Hyden	Susan Wheatley

Table of Contents

8 Time for You 199

Introduction

Picture this: Laura Petrie, tall, slim, and beautifully coifed, greets husband Rob just before his trip over the ottoman. Buddy and Sally rush over, laughing, as Rob completes his somersault, jumps to his feet, and, grinning broadly, shakes hands all around.

This is a man who's *worked* all day? There have been days when I would've just given up and stayed right there on the floor. "Day's over, I'm not moving," I'd say, and poor Laura would have to bring me dinner in the living room.

When Richie comes into the picture, he's greeted with warm smiles and attentive ears. No one's had a bad day. No one is so rushed that he hears, "Not now, Rich!" three times for every one, "What was it you wanted to tell me?" He's the pet of the Petrie household, and life, career, and family all seem to mix well.

Life in the '90s isn't much like a "Dick Van Dyke Show" episode. (It probably wasn't like that in the '60s, either.) Sometimes career and family mix about as well as oil and water. We have so many demands on our time that we struggle continually to prioritize our priorities. People get lost in the shuffle. Hurried and harried, we make choices that affect our lives—our earning potential, our futures, our families—before we really even understand that they *are* choices.

The Working Parents' Handbook is all about finding a balance—a workable balance—between home and office. No matter how harried you feel, there's hope. It *is* possible to have a career and kids at the same time; many of us are already doing it. How well we do it depends in large part on whether we've determined our family priorities, found a job that supports those priorities, and organized ourselves and our families to make sure we're headed toward the goals we want to reach.

Idealistic, perhaps, but not impossible.

Who Is This Book For?

The Working Parents' Handbook is a common-sense guide that bridges an important gap: the gap between home and work. If you're a parent who is considering a return to the workforce, a parent who has never worked and now has to, a parent who's in the market for a better job, a single parent shouldering both family and financial responsibilities, or a prospective parent considering the pros and cons of the life-career-baby triangle, you'll find insights, advice, practical information, and usable tips to help you sort out what's best for your family and for yourself.

In other words, if you are or will be a parent and you work, this book is for you.

What's in This Book?

Chapter 1, "Priorities, Priorities," gives you some basic information about what's happening today in American families and how other families are making it work. This chapter also presents tips for having a family discussion, weeding out the wants from the whining, determining your family's priorities, and designing a constructive family mission statement.

Chapter 2, "**Outside Looking In**," explores the point at which the needs of your family and the demands of the work world intersect. In this chapter you will rate various factors to identify the kind of job you want. How much do you need to make? How many hours can you be away? What benefits do you need? What about room for advancement? This chapter helps you weigh options and compare what you find with what your family needs. It also offers tips on conducting your job search and finding a "family-friendly" company.

Chapter 3, "**The Child-Care Issue**," addresses one of the biggest hurdles for most parents, especially those returning to the workforce for the first time as parents. Who can you trust to care for your children while you're at work? This chapter explores the options, from home-run day care to corporate-sponsored child care to grandma's house. There are other options, as well: the home office, the Mom-Dad-swing-shift circus act, and job sharing. This chapter helps you investigate all the choices and offers tips and checklists to help you make prepared decisions.

Chapter 4, "**Your Sitter Is on Line 1**," answers such questions as, How do you handle the first "Suzanne-just-threw up-on-the-family-room-carpet!" phone call? Should you run right home? How do you know when an emergency is an emergency? This chapter includes guidelines for responding to various situations from the office, and helps you prepare for emergencies *before* they happen.

Chapter 5, "**Inside Looking Out**," maps out that big first step: out the front door and into the office, and helps you navigate those trying first days with advice from other parents who've been there.

Chapter 6, "**Post-Parting Blues**," helps you gear up for the adjustment period ahead. Remember when you had that family meeting and designed your mission statement? Remember when everyone was happy to voice an opinion? Now, nobody's talking. Everyone's grumpy. The kids are getting sick. You're getting sick. You try to cover up the grayness you feel when you go to work, but you're afraid it shows. This chapter helps you understand what you're all going through and offers suggestions from experts on how to get back on course and stay there.

Chapter 7, "**On the Home Front**," deals with a common scenario: the house is going to pot! Your kids can write their names in the cat hair on the sofa. Three-meals' worth of dishes are piled in the sink. The trash is ripening in the garage because you forgot to put it out for the garbage pickup. Your home, once manageable, has become an unkempt reminder of how overly busy you are. This chapter helps you organize, prioritize, and delegate responsibilities so the necessary jobs get done. You'll find tips for chore sheets and allowance scales. Write-in calendars are provided so you can regiment important household tasks.

Chapter 8, "**Time for You**," helps you attempt the impossible: finding time for yourself. Maybe it's not logical, but it is fact: The more demands that are placed on your time, the more time you need to regroup. This chapter shows you how to grab some centering time and—even in the midst of a hectic schedule—take care of you. You can also reduce your stress and the demands on your time by taking charge of the dinnertime crazies and simplifying your responsibilities.

Chapter 9, "**Creating a Family-Friendly Workspace**," helps you become a family advocate even in the office. Many employers today recognize that, in order for their employees to be happy and excel at work, things must be okay at home; which means that many employers now offer a number of options to help support the work-family split. They are building on-site day-care centers, giving tuition assistance for preschools, and being more flexible about flex-time. This chapter tells you about what's being done to support families in the workplace and encourages you to explore what you can do in your office—from starting a parents-lunch-out once a month to putting up a parents' Q&A board where employees can find numbers for back-up baby-sitters, trade home-organizing tips, or arrange schedule swapping.

Appendixes

The final section of the book provides three quick references for additional information. Appendix A is a "Back-to-Work Checklist" that helps you hit all the major points before you start out that first day of work. Appendix B is a list of "Emergency Numbers for Home and Work." Appendix C closes the book with a listing of "Family-Friendly Resources," agencies and organizations dedicated to educating, empowering, and facilitating the growth of family-friendly workplaces.

Special Features

As we began researching this book, one fact became clear: Working parents are trying, and trying hard. Many of them have stories, tips, and suggestions to share. In this book, you'll find the voices of your peers—parents who are navigating uncharted waters, always with the best interest of their families at heart. Look for these special elements:

BEST & WORST BEST & **WORST**

Best & Worst
Parents tell you what they think are the best—and worst—aspects of being a working parent.

Did I Tell You About the Time . . . ?
These include stories—funny and sometimes poignant—parents have shared.

From One Parent to Another
These are tips parents offer from tried-and-true experience.

TIP

NOTE

NOTEPAD

PICK-UP
TIP

HOUSEHOLD
TIP

Additionally, you'll find tips, notes, sidebars, and checklists that provide information to support the chapter text and give you a chance to try out some of the recommended techniques. Household tips and pick-up tips in chapter 7 show how you can streamline your housekeeping efforts. Plus, we've thrown in some illustrations, just to keep things rolling.

Chapter

1

Priorities, Priorities

"When I was a kid, my parents moved a lot—but I always found them."
—Rodney Dangerfield

It's a staggering statistic: 77 million of us living in America today are parents. We represent a rainbow of ethnic backgrounds, educational levels, incomes, ages, and occupations. We have an incredible range of financial, emotional, practical, and physical needs. As you are ushering your 3-year-old out the door with her blanket and bunny, trying to get her into her car seat, thousands of parents just like you are doing the same thing all over the country. We all get those semi-hysterical phone calls from Grandma when Bradley swallows the cap to the glue. We all face sick days when we're not sick, and we all navigate the teacher-conference-or-managers'-meeting decisions.

The Balancing Act

Family consciousness is not a new thing, but it *is* speaking with a louder voice than it was a decade ago. Today more and more parents in the workforce are willing to exchange high-demand, high-stress careers for more holistically appealing lives. They want to go to PTA meetings once in a while. They want to make the cookies for the Boy Scout troop. They want to be the ones taking the baby's temperature and sponging her forehead when the flu hits and she really wants Mommy or Daddy.

In some cases, parents are willing to make a trade—less money, perhaps, or less responsibility in return for more freedom to be with their families. In other cases, the trade isn't necessary: Some do find jobs that enable them to set the priorities most important to them and balance work and home. The first step is setting the priorities.

Priority setting is a fairly simple task: You think about what's important to you as a family, discuss it, debate it if necessary, and decide. Voilà. Priorities. The challenge to setting your family priorities is finding the time to think about them. And anyone who's ever had a child to care for knows how unrealistic *that* can seem.

Early Mornings for Mom and Dad

As long as there have been jobs and kids, there have been parents trying to figure out how to balance the two. On a purely practical level, the chore is often close to impossible. Does this sound familiar?

6:00   Alarm rings. You hit the snooze button.

6:15   Alarm rings again. "Mom? Dad?" No, it's not the alarm. It's the kids.

6:20   One of you gets to shower; the other makes coffee. Hopefully you'll have time to switch places.

6:30   You break up a fight in the second bathroom. "Justin, you don't need to use Diana's curling iron."

7:00   Breakfast in concert. One makes lunches while the other serves cereal and Pop-Tarts.

7:10   Little Michael spills his juice. Again. Diana, trying to be helpful, grabs the closest thing she can get her hands on to mop it up. The closest thing happens to be the draft of the report you were working on last night.

7:20   Diana barely scoots out the door in time to catch the bus to junior high. Glancing down, you see she's forgotten her lunch. You'll have to drop it off on your way to the office.

7:30   Michael is still on his fourth spoonful of cereal. You bite your lip and try not to jump up and down screaming, "Hurry up! Hurry up!"

7:45   Your spouse is all packed and ready, with Justin and his bookbag waiting by the door. It's your turn to take Michael to preschool. A quick kiss, and they leave. Michael works on his seventh bite of cereal.

7:46   You can't stand it anymore. "Mike, I've got to get to the office on time today, and I've got to drop off Diana's lunch on my way. Are you just about finished eating?"

"Nunh-uh," Michael mumbles, chewing slowly.

You decide to be proactive. "Here," you say, "Let's take this Pop-Tart in the car. I know what I said about not eating in the new car, but we won't tell the other kids, okay? Come on—oh, we forgot to brush your teeth. Well, just remember to brush them twice as long tonight, all right?"

Picking up your briefcase (with the damp report inside) and scooping up Michael (with his tightly clutched Pop-Tart), you head for the door, destined to be at least 15 minutes late, even if traffic is smooth and you catch all the lights green.

Office Hours for Mom and Dad

By the time you get to the office, you're probably glad to be there. The meeting has started without you, so you pop open your briefcase, pull out the soggy report, and head down the hall toward the conference room. You pause at the door, take a deep breath, and walk in, smiling and as confident as possible. You've only missed a few minutes and are able to give your report and answer questions from the department managers. Much to your relief, things seem to go well, despite the morning's shaky start. After the meeting, your boss walks up. "A few of the managers asked for a copy of your report. Would you make a few copies and circulate them?"

"Uh, how about if I send them a copy by e-mail?" you ask, glancing down at the milk-stained report.

"That's fine," she says. She leans closer and points to your shoulder. "Um ... you have red streaks on your shirt...."

You glance down in horror. Cherry Pop-Tart. Thanks, Michael.

Of course, we bring with us to the office more than Pop-Tart fingerprints and milk-stained reports. We bring worries about sick children, day-care arrangements, upcoming doctor's appointments, and missed teacher conferences. Some of us bring guilt, too. And many of us never quite escape that torn feeling—that we should somehow be both at home and at work, care-taking and providing, doing it all.

Learn Those Lessons Well

Even the best parents are sometimes beset by doubts and guilts. Experts tell us that the quality—and, to some degree, the quantity—of the time we spend with our children is important. And we can rest assured that our presence in the workforce teaches our children some valuable lessons they might not otherwise learn:

- Our children learn about teamwork and cooperation.

- They learn how to set priorities.

- They discover how to make decisions.

- They develop an understanding of money.

- They find out about—and feel good about—what they have to offer the family.

- They see responsibility modeled in adults and learn to be responsible at home and at school.[1]

How Is America Parenting?

Parenting is hard work even when you aren't responsible for merging two different cultures, age groups, perspectives, and lifestyles. The switch back and forth from the work world to home life is akin to culture shock for many of us: We often go from Wall Street to "Sesame Street" in a matter of minutes.

In his study *Parents in Modern America: A Sociological Analysis*, done in the early 1970s, researcher E. E. LeMasters found that there are 13 characteristics all American parents share, no matter what ethnic, religious, educational, or financial group they belong to.[2] You'll probably recognize some of your challenges here:

1. We aren't sure what a "good parent" is. The role is ambiguous at best. It's up to each of us to decide for ourselves what successful parenting means.

2. We expect to be able to solve problems even professionals cannot.

3. Except for Lamaze classes (which don't help a whole lot when you're facing a 13-year-old who's cutting school) we get no formal parenting training.

4. Perhaps because we aren't realistically pre-pared, we have romantic ideas of parenting.

5. We have complete responsibility for our chil-dren but only partial authority.

6. We place extremely high standards on our-selves and on one another as parents.

7. We often must work with incomplete or con-flicting information in deciding how to resolve situations with our children.

8. We do not choose our children, which means we are responsible whether we want to be or not!

9. We have no models to follow for parenting in the '90s. We've been swayed this way and that by popular culture and the method of the moment, but each generation changes so much in its parenting styles that we are inventing the model as we go.

10. Although this may be the dawn of the family-friendly age, economics is still the bottom line. We must earn a living to be able to provide for our children, which sets the stage for some necessary trade-offs.

11. With the continued rise in the number of two-income families, we are adding more roles that compete with the demanding role of parenting.

12. Parenting is a no-quit endeavor. If you don't like your job, you can quit. If you don't like a movie, you can leave. If you don't like your spouse—well, I won't tell you what to do about your spouse. But once a parent, always a parent—for better *and* for worse.

13. The standards we set for our children are higher even than the bar we set for ourselves as parents. We want our children to do better, to have more, to be happier and more successful in life than we are. That's a pretty tall order—both for ourselves and for our kids.

BEST &
WORST

Best:
"Knowing
I'm
providing
for my
kids"

How Is America Working?

The responses families come up with to make their home lives work are as varied as their parenting styles and occupational circumstances. The following sections briefly review some of the different ways families balance work and home.

Two Parents, Two Careers

Many of us parenting today were raised very differently than our parents were. Before World War II, life was closer to "Ozzie and Harriet"; it's likely that our mothers were raised by mothers who stayed home and parented for a living. Such families are in the minority today. These days, all kinds of factors—the cost of living, the pursuit of self-fulfillment, societal pressures—contribute to our needs and desires to work outside the home.

The term *two-career family* covers many different arrangements. One parent might be the primary provider, while the other works part-time. Perhaps both parents are necessary breadwinners. Or one parent might work two jobs while the other works either full- or part-time.

Two-career families—especially those in which both parents work full-time—face unique challenges because of the conflicting demands placed on their limited time. There is much to be done, and there are only 24 hours in a day. Organization is mandatory. Teamwork is essential.

For practical how-to's and wherefore's on getting and keeping your house organized and your team members enlisted, see chapter 7.

One Parent, One Career

Statistics tell us that 31 percent of all households with children are currently headed by single parents—which means a single income—and single mothers outnumber single fathers 6 to 1.[3]

If you are the sole provider for your family, you face additional challenges. You are navigating work and family responsibilities without the support of another adult to share the load. For you, organization and teamwork—in this case, enlisting the help of your children—are supremely important. They can make the difference between you and yours being harried or happy.

According to a study published in Working Mother *magazine, a divorced mother's job has a positive effect on her children.[4] Research shows that families headed by working mothers tend to join in more recreational activities together, and that the children have a solid basis of self-esteem—perhaps because of the additional financial stability in the family or the mother's increased confidence and independence.*

Two Parents, One Career

The "traditional" family of the 1950s—June Cleaver, *et al.*—was represented by the male head-of-household, the female homemaker, and the young, carefree offspring. The '90s version of the traditional family is different. The working-outside-the-home parent may be Mom or Dad—or Mom *and* Dad. If one parent does stay home, he or she may do the carpool thing, the child-care thing, or the work-at-home thing.

Even in a two-parent, single-career family, there is balancing to be done. Both parents are still parents, after all. The parents are partners financially and emotionally, and the prioritizing and organization of the family are still important.

Alternatives

We've looked at some of the more obvious categories of working parents. But there are other options to be explored. Depending on what is most important to your family, you may want to think about one of these alternatives:

Working Different Shifts

According to the *Statistical Abstract of the United States 1995*, 17.8 percent of workers currently work shifts other than traditional daytime hours: 5.1 percent work the evening shift; 3.7 percent work nights; and 3.4 percent work a rotating shift—some days, some evenings, some nights.[5]

For families that place a priority on child care by Mom or Dad, this offsetting of shifts works well, especially while the kids are young. But the challenges are obvious, and parents have to make "couple time" a priority to keep this relationship happy and healthy.

Working at Home

Another growing segment of our parenting population is working at home. With computer technology and the ability to link home and office easily by modem, more employers are open to complete or partial work-at-home arrangements.

◆ ◆ ◆ ◆ ◆ ◆ ◆ ◆ ◆ ◆ ◆ ◆ ◆ ◆

*"I'm home all day with my
3-year-old while my
husband works. I start
dinner about 4:00, and
when Tom gets home at
5:15, I leave for work.
When I get home at 1:30,
he's asleep. I go to bed
and when I wake up,
Tom's already left for
work. We aren't seeing
each other much right
now—I figure we've got
another year or so of
this—but at least we're
able to raise Jonathan the
way we want to."*

◆ ◆ ◆ ◆ ◆ ◆ ◆ ◆ ◆ ◆ ◆ ◆ ◆ ◆

Some work-at-home parents are
entrepreneurs; others have
arrangements with
their employers to
work one or
more days a
week at home
and still be
eligible for
benefits and
other perks of
employment.

Statistically, 3.2 percent of
men and 3.5 percent of women
in the workforce—parents or
not—are working at home an
average of 14.1 hours a week.[6]

From One Parent to Another
*"If you miss your kids like I do, try to
start a business in your home. Then you
can earn some extra money, raise your
kids the way you want, and not have the
expense of baby-sitters and/or day care."*
—Mother of two who works more than full-time

Setting Your Priorities

As you can see, there are many ways to balance
the home-family equation. You may come up with
something original, or you may try one or two
different alternatives before you settle into a
situation that really works for your family.

The first step is to go on a fact-finding mission:
What are the priorities for your family? What are

your goals? What's most important to you as a family, and to you as an individual?

Determining your family priorities is an important step in the process of balancing home and work. You must decide what you're working toward before you can begin moving toward it. Finding out what your family priorities are involves these steps:

1. Talk with your spouse to determine what your priorities are from a parental and financial-partnering standpoint.

2. Have a family meeting in which you invite— and record—input from all family members.

3. Review the list of priorities with your spouse and edit it into a family priority list.

4. Call a second family meeting and read the family priority list. From the list, write a family mission statement—a simple statement that explains what your family wants most to accomplish. Post the mission statement, along with household rules and chore lists (we'll get to those in chapter 7), on the family bulletin board.

Starting Out

The first step in determining your family priorities involves the parents in the house. If you are a single parent, you can sit down with a notebook and a pen and get right to work. If you have a partner, arrange a quiet time when the kids are busy or in bed, when you can have 30 minutes to an hour to talk uninterrupted.

Talking about family priorities cuts right to the heart of family life—why we married, what we wanted, who we've become, who we want to be, how we're raising our kids—and should be handled with gentleness and respect. Take as much time as you can—preferably a long, quiet evening or, even better, a weekend away—to focus on what's important to you as individuals, as a couple, and as a family. Don't try to squeeze in a quick discussion after a tough day at the office or at half-time during your daughter's basketball game.

Brainstorm a list of priorities—whatever comes to you—in no particular order. Don't force yourself to think of what is most important and then list other things in degrees of lesser importance. Just ask yourself (or your mate) "What's important for this family?" and write down whatever comes to mind. You can prioritize the items—and probably throw out a few and add others—when you go through the list later.

As you go through this brainstorming process, here are a few things to keep in mind:

 Different families will have different priorities, and those priorities will change as your children get older, as your financial needs increase or decrease, or as other opportunities present themselves.

 Don't expect your priorities and your partner's priorities to be identical. Go into the discussion expecting negotiation and compromise. If you think it's most important to get out of debt within two years and she thinks it's most important to have at least one parent home with the kids most of the time, that doesn't mean one of you is right and the other is wrong. What you're working on is not a list of your own priorities that everyone else in the family should fall in line with, but a collection of priorities that everyone agrees to (with the parents having the lion's share of the say).

 Everything counts. Write down whatever comes into your head at this stage, no matter how trivial. "Clean laundry" may not be high up on your priorities list, but if it occurs to you, write it down.

 Don't judge your partner's comments. If Sam says "Changing the oil in the riding mower" is one of the family priorities, write it down. There will be time for editing later. Just keep the ideas moving, and don't negate anything your partner finds important.

A Few Possible Family Priorities

To be debt-free in five years

To create a loving, happy home

To spend time every week alone with each child

To reserve one evening a week for ourselves as a couple

To be able to purchase a house

To save for our children's college education

To be able to take a family vacation once a year

To purchase a new van

To be more active at church or in civic organizations

Having a Family Discussion

Once you have your parental list, the next step is to add the voices of the kids. What do they think is most important for your family? Their input is important, both for the perspective it will give you and for their need to be included in decisions that affect them and will ultimately require their support.

Including the kids in the discussion ensures that they feel part of the process: So when it's their turn to do the dishes and they'd rather watch TV, they understand the "whys" behind the chores and realize—somewhere deep down, underneath the compensatory grumbling—that everyone is doing his or her part to make sure the family's priorities are being honored.

Don't just spring a surprise family meeting on the kids. Make it an event. Publicize it. Order pizza, rent a movie (for afterward), do something special. Explain a few days before the meeting what you want to talk about—"We want to hear what you think is most important for our family"—so your kids have a chance to think about it on their own before the meeting. Remember, nobody thinks well on a pop quiz.

When you call the family meeting to order, don't expect absolute order. The first time I tried to have a family meeting with my three children, I made the mistake of doing it at dinner. My teenager made three or four cynical comments. My 7-year-old shouted out things like, "My bedtime is too early! I want to watch 'Beetlejuice' in the mornings, and you won't let me! Cameron drives me crazy!" And Cameron, the baby, threw his mashed potatoes on the carpet. I gave up and dejectedly went to get the carpet cleaner. Weeks passed before I drummed up the nerve to try again. With more thoughtful planning, and a more controlled environment, things went much more smoothly.

For best results, have an agenda. As the saying goes (and it is especially applicable with kids), "Act or be acted upon." Have a sense of humor about it, but get your point across: "Kids, you know I'm thinking about going back to work (or changing jobs, or whatever), and we're trying to decide what's most important for our family so we can make sure we're all happy and cared for while these changes are going on. We want to hear what's most important to you, and what you think is most important for our family."

You might be surprised at what you hear. Again, don't judge the answers, just write them down. If someone isn't talking, ask. "Bethany, what do you think is the most important thing in a family? What do you think is important for you to be happy?" Depending on the age of the child, she may or may not know the answer. (Some of us still haven't figured it out!) But whatever she says— even if she says nothing at all—you've let her know that her feelings are important and welcome as part of this family process. You're enlisting her understanding and participation—even if she's too young to really understand what's going on.

A Few Child-Offered Priorities

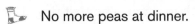 No more peas at dinner.

I want Mom to play Sega with me more often.

New jeans.

Cartoons.

I want to go out with my friends more.

My own room.

Drums.

 A later bedtime.

 Someone else to take out the trash.

After you write down the various priorities, wants, and needs that come raining down on you, take time to read back what you've written. Ask for clarification if you're not sure what was meant. "Bethany, you said 'dinner' was important. Did you mean just having it, or having it together as a family?" Make sure you understand what your kids think is important, even if you don't share their views. Remember, you're gathering facts here. You and your spouse (or just you, if you're a single parent) get to make the final cuts, taking everyone's wants and needs into consideration.

Separating Wants from Whining

Some of what you hear will be helpful. Some will be confusing. And some will be veiled—or perhaps not so veiled—attempts to make you feel guilty and give in to some privilege you have previously denied.

In our house, television is not a high priority. It especially is not a high priority for me, the Keeper of the TV Control. When Christopher tells me he needs to watch a particular cartoon in order to feel loved and happy, I file that comment in the "whining" category. He's pushing my buttons and that gets a parental veto. When he says it's important that I stay and watch during his Taekwondo class instead of dropping him off and running errands, I understand that he wants my involvement. He wants me to be proud of him, and he doesn't like to be dropped off. That comment I record as a want that is important and something I'll consider in the future.

We all know there's a fine line between direct communication and manipulation. Where that line is in your family only you can know for sure. As you gather the information for your family priority list, however, don't leave anything out—even if you think it's manipulative. Just write it all down, and weed out the sneaky stuff later.

BEST &
WORST

Worst:
"Finding time to attend school functions"

Editing the List

Now it's time for you and your partner in parenting to sit down and sift through the list you've compiled. Read through it individually once or twice; then go through it point by point. Some items you'll be able to consolidate; others you will want to omit. And you may think of others to add.

You may find your priorities falling into three general categories:

Financial

Emotional

Physical

Please note that Financial is listed first, not because it is more important than the emotional or physical needs of the family, but because it is more difficult to address the other needs when the family is in a state of financial crisis. Most of us return to the workforce at least in part for financial reasons. Additional financial benefits can make working with emotional and physical needs easier. And, on the flip side, emotional and physical needs can definitely be magnified in times of financial strain.

After you've thought about your family priorities and reached some kind of consensus, take a moment and fill out the Priority List provided at the end of this chapter.

Here's a sample priority list showing how the items are organized once the list is compiled and condensed:

Family Priority List

Financial Priorities
To add a new family room next spring.
To get Christine a car for her 16th birthday.
To save 10 percent of our annual salaries.

Emotional Priorities
To create an atmosphere of love, safety, and acceptance.
To cooperate with each other to help our household
   run smoothly.
To value the feelings of each family member.
To listen to each other.
To be willing to voice our opinions.
To respect others' opinions.

Physical Priorities
To be warm, safe, and cared for.
To be well fed.
To have comfortable, acceptable, and season-
   appropriate clothing.
To take good care of ourselves and stay as healthy
   as possible.
To follow household safety rules at all times.

One very important point: Now that you've
created your priority list, you've got the basic
information you need to make some important
decisions about how to approach your work
options. Remember, however, that every system
needs to be reviewed and revised on a regular
basis, and your family priority list is no exception.
You will find that some things that are priorities
now will drop off the list in the coming months
and other priorities will arise. Be willing to review

and revise whenever you see that a change is
needed. Your family grows and changes
continually, and so will their priorities and needs.

Did I Tell You About the Time . . . ?

*"When our youngest daughter was 2, I
asked the pharmacist if Stresstabs really
worked. He said they did, and I was
overjoyed. Curious at my reaction, he asked
what kind of stress I was talking about. I replied, '2-
year-old, toddler stress!' He said, 'Oh, no, ma'am.
Stresstabs work for muscle stress, not mental stress! I
think what you're looking for are tranquilizers!'"*
                                  —Mother of two who works part-time

---

Developing a Mission Statement

Now that you've determined what's most
important to your family, you need to distill it
down to a single mission statement that says
clearly what you want to accomplish as a family.
Do this in a group meeting. (Yes, I can hear your
10-year-old now: "Not *another* family meeting! I
want to watch 'The Simpsons!'") Just one more
time.

Take your priority list and read it aloud to the kids.
Explain that you want to reduce the list to a
simple statement about what's most important.
Ask for input, and write the statement right there
on the spot.

One family may focus more on emotional issues—
feeling loved, safe, supported, accepted—while
another may focus on practical issues—taking care
of the house, getting out of debt, cooperating and
getting along. There's no right or wrong, there's
only what's most important for your family.

Here are a few examples:

 "Our mission as a family is to create an environment in which all family members feel loved, safe, and cared for."

 "Our mission as a family is to work together to create a loving, safe, and beautiful home."

 "Our mission as a family is to cooperate and help each other with the daily running of the household."

 "Our mission as a family is to encourage, strengthen, challenge, and support each other as we learn the lessons in our lives."

 "Our mission as a family is to work together to improve our financial situation so we can build the home we've always wanted."

Posting It

Well congratulate yourself, you've done it. You've made the change from reactive family living—that is, reacting to whatever situation comes along—to proactive family living—deciding what's important to you and making your decisions based on those priorities. You may or may not see the change right away, but it will be at the basis of every family decision you make, in terms of job hunting, chore assigning, or goal setting. Underneath it all, you'll know your family's mission statement— what's most important to you and why—and you'll be able to make your choices accordingly.

Family Priority List

Date: __ / __ / __

Financial Priorities

_____

_____

_____

_____

Emotional Priorities

_____

_____

_____

_____

Physical Priorities

_____

_____

_____

_____

Family Mission Statement

Date: __/__/__

Our mission as a family is to

_____

_____

_____

_____

Notes

1. Earl A. Grollman and Gerri L. Sweder, *The Working Parent Dilemma* (Boston: Beacon Press, 1983).

2. J. Ross Eshleman, *The Family: An Introduction* (Englewood Cliffs, NJ: Allyn & Bacon, 1974), pp. 511-512.

3. *The World Almanac 1995* (Mahwah, NJ: Funk & Wagnalls), p. 960.

4. *Working Mother* magazine (September 1995).

5. *Statistical Abstract of the United States 1995*, Tables 635 & 636.

6. Ibid.

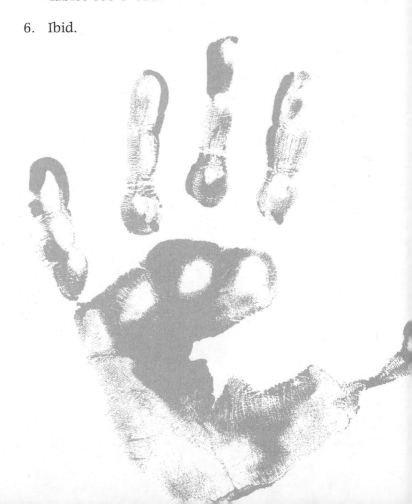

2

Outside Looking In

A man was late for work. *"What's the idea of being late?"* asked the boss.

"Well, the alarm clock woke up everybody but me this morning."

"What do you mean, the alarm clock woke up everybody in the family but you?"

"Well, there's eight in our family and the clock was set for seven."
—Ed Ford

This chapter is all about finding the right job, the one that uses your talents and meets both your needs and the needs of your family. First we'll

take a look at what you decided is important for
your family. Then we'll come up with a list of
essentials for the "perfect" job. (I'm not promising
that you'll find the perfect job right off the bat, but
you have a lot better chance of finding it if you've
figured out what it is.)

Maybe you already have a job and are
reconsidering whether you've made the right
choice or whether it's time for a different one:
Statistics show that 44 percent of all working
adults expect to be looking for a different job
within the next three years.[1] Or you may be
preparing to enter or reenter the workforce. In
any case, coming at your job search from the
"What's the right job for our family?" standpoint
will help you find something that aligns with what
is important in your life.

Stress-Busters

Looking for a job can be a full-time occupation. In
fact, experts agree that the more focus and follow-
up you're willing to invest in your job search, the
more likely you are to get the job you want. When
you add family responsibilities to the sometimes
complex and often harrowing experience of
looking for work, the result is often an extra
helping of stress and a shortage of patience.

For that reason, let's start out with a few job search
stress-busters.

 **Remember that everything doesn't have
to be done right now.** When you feel the
pressure to mail out 20 resumes, *and* write
follow-up letters, *and* make those phone
calls, *and* you're late for Todd's basketball
practice, *and* Dana's bugging you to use the
phone, stop before you see red and breathe.
Five or six good, deep breaths will do it.
Remind yourself that finding a job—like
raising children—takes a steady investment
of time, and the kinder you can be with

yourself in the process, the better. Your family will thank you for it.

 Keep things as organized as you can. Set up a job search work area in a corner of the family room, the den, or a home office where people won't make off with the paper, where your daughter won't color on the backs of your resumes, and your 3" by 5" note cards won't get shuffled or shredded into doilies.

 Create a schedule for yourself that works with your family responsibilities. We all know how hard it is to grab time for ourselves, but when you're looking for work, it's imperative. Schedule time for reviewing want ads, making phone calls, writing follow-up letters, creating interview cards, and so on. Break these activities up to do at different times of the day, if you need to, but schedule them. You'll know you are accomplishing your goals, and the extra planning will help you look forward to the next step.

 Review your progress at the end of the week. Keep a record each day (preferably in a day-planner or on a calendar) of who you contacted, when, what the result was, and what action you need to take. At the end of the week, go back and review all the contacts you made. Take time to honor the investment of brainpower, willpower, and energy it took to make all those connections and push yourself forward. That will give you the incentive (after a day or two off) to start fresh on Monday.

 Learn to let it rest. Especially when it's a financial bind that is causing a sudden search for work, the temptation to get all caught up in the job search is very strong. As creatures of habit, we humans think only one thing at a time; and when that one thing has to do with money (especially a shortage of it), we can easily get obsessive. If you find yourself constantly thinking of your job search and your money situation, hold up a mental stop sign and look around you. Those kids over there, fighting over the TV, they'd rather play a game with you than hear about the frustrations of your job search. Your friend next door would surely like some help putting that wallpaper border up straight this time. There are many things in our lives besides our most current and most upsetting worry. We just need to remember to see them.

What Does Your Family Need?

In the last chapter, you came up with a family list of priorities that took into account what you and your partner (or you, yourself, if you're a single parent) feel is most important for your family's goals to be met. You solicited input from the kids, as well, making sure they knew they were included and welcomed as you developed both the priority list and your family's mission statement.

You should have a pretty good idea by now of what's important to your family and what isn't. That's going to be different for everyone, so there's no general guideline to follow on what works and what doesn't. Your list, whatever it says, and your mission statement will be your guiding factors when you're considering what your family needs as you find the job to match. But this brings up another question.

What About You?

Searching for a job is, after all, a singular undertaking. We don't look for jobs in groups (at least most people don't). The ideal job for you is going to be one that uses your talents, that gives you room to grow, that meets the needs of your family, and that gives you a sense of satisfaction.

Notice that *"meets the needs of your family"* is only one part of the equation.

Perhaps the best advice I ever heard on job searching is something a friend said to me a few years ago: "Spend a few minutes visualizing yourself in the place you're thinking about working. If you see yourself miserable and glum, forget it. If you see yourself contented and happy, consider it. If you see yourself frazzled and stressed out, run the other way!"

In other words, no matter what kind of situation you're up against, taking a job that makes you miserable is not going to help your family. Part of finding the right job for your family involves finding the right job for you: A happier you means a more supportive, funny, available parent, which translates into better times with the kids.

One mother whose two boys wanted her to "get them everything" for Christmas, answered this way:

"I asked them if they'd rather me work full-time so they could have more things, or would they rather me be home most of the time and just settle for fewer Christmas gifts. They quickly replied they'd much rather me be home with them."

Later in this chapter, you'll have a chance to identify some of the things that are most important to you in a job. The job you want is out there. You just need to know what you're looking for, so you know it when you find it.

These are the things I like to do:

1. _____
2. _____
3. _____
4. _____
5. _____
6. _____
7. _____
8. _____
9. _____
10. _____

What Do You Want to Keep?

When you begin looking for work, one thing is certain: Life is going to change. At first the kids may not believe it. Even though you did the family priority list thing and the mission statement, the idea that "Mom is going back to work" or "Dad is changing jobs" may not have sunk in. You might be asking for more help around the house so you can spend time on your job search. You might need the phone more (that will be *really* unpopular with your teenager), but the reality of "what's changing around here" won't seem real at first.

Before you start making sweeping changes, take a quiet look around—perhaps for a week or so—and see what works and what doesn't. I speak here from the experience of having used the wrong approach for years. I did everything around the house myself until a pressing deadline turned me into a stressed-out lunatic. I knew I was going about things the wrong way when my 14-year-old said, "Mom, the next time you go to the store, could you get me a new toothbrush?"

It was too much. "A new toothbrush?" I asked, incredulously. "A new toothbrush? Didn't I just get you one last month?"

She shrugged. The bicycle chain around her neck jangled. (Don't ask, it's the new look.) "I lost it," she mumbled.

"Lost it? How do you lose a toothbrush? Well, in a room like yours, I can see how. Why don't you ever clean that room? And how come I'm the only one who ever cleans up anything around here? You'd think that as hard as I work, you kids ... "

And I was off. My daughter's eyes glazed and she glanced toward the nearest exit.

Luckily, I stopped myself before I started foaming at the mouth and they had to call in the Tranquilizer Squad. Thank goodness—for myself and my kids—those outbursts are rare events.

Here's the point: An ounce of prevention is worth a pound of cure. If I'd looked around my house in a moment of relative calm—or at least without the job search (or deadline) stress weighing on me—I would have seen that, yes, Christopher brings in the trash cans on Tuesdays and, okay, Kelly has been doing the dishes like I asked her to. They are helping. Where could they do more?

And when I calmly answered that question for myself, I could think about how to implement it without ranting, "Why don't you help more?" Instead, I could say, very politely, "This is what we all need to do to chip in and make this household work."

Ah ... much better.

What Will Have to Change?

If you're a parent, odds are you've said it: "There are only so many hours in the day!" If you're a parent who is working or who is contemplating returning to the workforce, you know that time is like money: we always need or want more and are never quite sure where it will come from.

If you are preparing for a return to work, you know things around the house will change. Already, as you gather your job search tools, think about contacts, read the papers, and talk to relatives, there are more demands on your time than ever before. When you find the job you're looking for, the demands on your time will be even greater. That's why now is a good time to think about what you'll want to change when you start working.

Some of the changes may be predicated on when and where you work. For example, if you work nights, you may need to have one of the older children help the younger children with bath time. Or if you have a long commute, you may need your spouse to start supper in the evening.

In this early stage, just looking around at what works now and what might need to change is the key. Make a list of who does what and file it away for the future family discussion on chore distribution (that's chapter 7).

Again, you may see things that you know will need to change—like the way Christopher throws his book bag and coat in the middle of the living room floor when he walks in from school. Tackle it now, if you want, but if you've got enough on your plate right now, write it in the "Needs to Change" column and institute it as a new rule at the next family meeting.

The Home Planner

Chore   Who Does It?

_____   _____

_____   _____

_____   _____

_____   _____

_____   _____

_____   _____

_____   _____

_____   _____

_____   _____

_____   _____

_____   _____

_____   _____

_____   _____

_____   _____

What Do We Need to Change?

_____

_____

_____

_____

_____

_____

_____

_____

_____

_____

_____

_____

_____

_____

_____

_____

_____

What's Out There?

The job force is expanding and changing every day. When our parents (or perhaps their parents) went to work, they were fairly certain that this would be the job they would hold for the rest of their lives. Jobs were almost exclusively performed on-site; there were few work-at-home occupations outside of home-service businesses and health-care professionals who made house calls.

BEST &
WORST

Best:
"Double
insurance
coverage"

Today, as Walt Disney said, "If you can dream it, you can do it." All kinds of opportunities are opening up in cottage industries, home businesses, or businesses that truly exist somewhere in the phone lines of cyberspace. Computers have made all kinds of services lucrative and possible for people who want to stay home and work. They also make it feasible for employers to hire people who divide their time between work in the office and work at home: If they can take their files back and forth, what difference does it make whether they sit at this desk or that one?

The Home-Office Split

Not all employers are thrilled with the loss of control involved in setting employees free to work at home. Many do so grudgingly, and over time see the benefit of a happy employee who is more productive because he's able to balance the priorities in his life.

Studies have shown that of the 110 million employees in the United States, 19 million of them do at least some of their work at home. The number is not terribly high, but getting higher. The average number of hours they work at home ranges from 12 to just under 17 hours a week.

Work at Home for Someone Else or for Yourself?

If you're thinking about working at home, you might wonder why you'd rather be someone else's employee when you could work for yourself. Many of us have wondered the same thing. The following lists touch on a few of the basic differences:

When you are working for someone else:

- You are usually home only part of the time (one or two days a week).

- You can still "leave the office at the office."

- You draw a regular paycheck.

- You are covered on the company health plan.

- Any benefits that apply to a full-time employee apply to you (assuming you're working full-time).

When you are working for yourself:

- You may have start-up costs ranging from minimal to substantial.

- You are your own boss, which means Discipline, Discipline, Discipline!

👢 Everything that happens is yours to deal with.

👢 You need to meet with an accountant and an attorney to get started on the right foot.

👢 You've got to have a sound idea for a business that you know will go.

In both cases, you still need a plan for making sure the kids are cared for. You will still have demands on your time, and there will still be competing demands for your attention.

The decision of whether to work for yourself or for someone else is one that many people wrestle with throughout their careers. If you're not sure what you want to do, the safer road is to find a job that allows you to work at home part of the time. That way, you can see how you respond to the work style (some people find they have trouble keeping work and home separate when they occupy the same space) and ease into it with a smaller degree of risk.

Job Sharing

Working out an arrangement in which you are at home part of the time is not the only way a parent can find a job style that fits his or her family's needs. Other alternatives exist, including job sharing. In job sharing, more than one employee shares the same job, thus enabling the employer to get the same amount of work done, and two employees to have jobs (and, in some cases, benefits) and still be able to orchestrate the priorities in their lives.

From One Parent to Another
"The most important gift you can give your child is a good set of values. Let your children live with the consequences of their mistakes when they are young, and the consequences are not as life-impacting later."
—Mother of two who works full-time

Seasonal Jobs

If your talents or interests lead you into seasonal
work, you have another option for the way you
mix work and family. Teaching is a somewhat
seasonal job that blends in well with family life—
although any teacher will tell you that the number
of hours spent working outside the classroom,
grading papers, writing lesson plans, and
designing projects, makes for a full-to-bursting
day. The schedule a teacher follows, however,
allows Mom or Dad to be home during the
summer and on Christmas and spring vacations, to
have relatively short work days (at least at-school
work days), and to have weekends off.

Other kinds of seasonal jobs include retail sales,
facility management, house painting, landscaping,
and construction.

If You Need Time Off

As you begin your job search, you should be aware that the
Family and Medical Leave Act was passed in 1993 to guarantee
up to 12 weeks of time off for family members in certain
situations. There are a few stipulations, though. Companies with
fewer than 50 employees are not required to follow FMLA
guidelines. All companies with more than 50 employees, and all
government agencies, are required to give you up to 12 weeks of
(usually unpaid) leave, although you may be able to work out
vacation or sick time you haven't used in order to arrange for
continuing salary. If you begin working for a company of 50 or
more (or a government agency), you are protected by the Family
and Medical Leave Act if you need to take time off for any of
these circumstances:

- The birth of a child

- The crisis care of an immediate family member

- The adoption of a child

- Your own medical condition that keeps you from
working

The FMLA applies to both women and men—moms and dads—and workers are guaranteed their same or equivalent positions when they return to work. If for some reason your position has been filled when you come back, you will be assigned a similar job with identical salary and benefits.

Setting Up Your Job Search

By now, you've spent some time thinking about the kind of job arrangement you'd like. Have you considered the type of job you'd like to have, the one that would use your talents and give you a chance to show what you can do? If not, a little brainstorming is in order.

In *The Very Quick Job Search* J. Michael Farr identifies six essential steps that will help you find the job you want quickly.[2]

1. **Know what you have to offer your employer.** What are your strengths? What can you bring to the job that someone else could not? Don't be afraid to give voice to your skills. That's not bragging, it's presenting yourself.

2. **Know what you want from a job.** Think of this in terms of both practicalities—type of work, location, people, pay—and personal accomplishments—challenge, creativity, advancement, opportunity.

If you aren't sure what kinds of jobs appeal to you, take a trip of the library and look through *America's Top 300 Jobs* or the *Occupational Outlook Handbook*.[3] These books will give you an overview of many of the jobs available in the United States today. Some may require additional education and/or training, but others won't.

3. **Know where to look.** Fewer than 15 percent of all jobs are found through ads in the newspaper. Where else is there? Contacts are everywhere, you just need to know where to find them. Friends, family, acquaintances—even your son's parent's friends or your daughter's troop leader—may be the links that lead you to the job you want.

See *The Very Quick Job Search* for a wealth of practical ideas on how to best find, organize, and act on your job leads.[4]

4. **Take your job search seriously.** Treat your job search like a job. Research shows that the harder you look for the job you want, the more likely it is you will find it quickly. Organize your job search information— books, resumes, papers, note cards, business cards, pens, calendars, day-planner—and put it in a Hands-Off! area of your home. Maybe it's in the kitchen; maybe it's a quiet spot in the den. Set up your area and put armed guards there if you have to, but protect it. No, Sam *doesn't* need to color on the back of your note cards. Treat your job search—and the tools you need to complete it—as seriously as you would any work assigned you by your future employer.

5. **Get out there.** Planning and researching aren't easy, but they don't involve too much risk. Most people dread the interview stage, where they are setting appointments and keeping them, and opening themselves up to possible judgment and—gulp!—rejection. But you won't get a job sitting in the house. Eventually, you have to get out there and interview.

The Very Quick Job Search has wonderful advice on how to make sure you don't get into a cat-and-mouse interview game: Make it a point to approach employers who aren't hiring.[5] They will be impressed with your foresight ("I know you're not hiring right now, but I'm really interested in your company and wanted to find out how I could submit my resume in case you have any openings...") and your initiative. The employer will not be looking for how you *don't* fit—as she might be if she's interviewing dozens of prospective employees—and will be more likely to see the strengths you could bring to the organization.

A Mental Health Minute

Sometimes—especially if you're returning to the workforce after several years of stirring Cream of Wheat—the hardest thing about the job search is opening the front door and walking out. You might feel that life has passed you by. Things you used to know are outdated. Things you hoped you'd know by now don't seem so important.

Okay, close the door. You're not quite ready yet. Get a pencil and a pad of paper, and make a list of all your strengths. I mean everything. If you're great with a can of cleanser, write it down. If you can sing like Pavarotti, write it down. If you've got computer skills or a good phone voice or don't get paper cuts easily, write it down. Fixing lawnmowers? It's a skill. Good at calming down your mother-in-law? It's a talent that will come in handy. Able to deliver three children to three different after-school activities and still have time to get the dog groomed? Believe me, that's a gift.

The point is that you've been doing things for years that you haven't necessarily seen as part of your skills set. Parenting is all about skills: people skills, management skills, coping skills, communication skills. There's literally nothing you've learned as a parent that won't translate in some useful way to your work.

When you've made your list, go get yourself a cup of coffee and look over the list long and hard. This is about you and what you have to offer. Be proud of it. All experience is useful experience, whether you've been paid for it monetarily or not. When you feel secure that what you have to offer an employer is *more* today than it was a few years ago *because of your experience*, go ahead and open the door and walk out. The world will be a better place for it.

---

6. **Keep in touch.** Once you've made the initial contact, whether it's a phone call, a dropped-off resume, or a full-blown interview, follow up. Send a thank-you card; wait a set period of time and follow up with a phone call. Get organized about your follow-ups, but make sure you don't let a contact drop until you're certain the position has been filled. And even if the decision was made for someone else, be pleasant about it and ask the employer to keep your resume on file. It's especially important not to burn bridges in the job world. You might be passing this way again someday.

Employer Possibilities

Here's a list of employers I'm interested in contacting:

1. _____
2. _____
3. _____
4. _____
5. _____
6. _____
7. _____
8. _____
9. _____
10. _____

What Can You Give Your Employer?

Somewhere in the back of your mind you should have a basic idea of what your family needs—financially, emotionally, and physically. Hopefully you've also spent some time thinking about the type of job that would make you happy: home or work, full-time or part-time, one that would enable you to use your hands or your brain—you get the idea.

One last step before you turn yourself loose on the world of prospective employers: Determine how far you're willing to go. What, in terms of hours and commitment, are you prepared to offer? Get a clear picture of this before you walk into that first interview, and you'll have not only a better chance of getting what you want but an increased probability that you'll recognize the "wrong" job right off the bat.

Defining "Can"

The word "can" can give us problems. In this context, the question "What can you give your employer?" does not mean "What is it humanly possible for you to give your employer?" but, rather, "In light of your family's priority list and mission statement, and taking into account the type of job you think would make you happy, what are you willing to give your employer?"

You "can" do all sorts of things. You can take a job because you feel you have to, right now (and sometimes those situations happen), and be miserable, underappreciated, and underpaid. You can work many more hours than you want to "for the money." You can show up when someone calls in sick, and you can frantically try to arrange for a baby-sitter on your days off when you're called in unexpectedly. You "can" do all those things.

What you're trying to do instead is be proactive about the type of job you select, so you get a job that fits what you and your family need, instead of taking a job "because you have to" and trying to make your family fit around it.

So consider what you're willing to invest in terms of time, commitment, and flexibility before you put that best foot forward. Being clear about what you want—and what you're offering—will help both you and your eventual employer make the right match.

Hours

Jobs come in all shapes and sizes, with all kinds of hourly commitments—from a few hours a week to nearly every waking moment. When you think about the hours you want to work, ask yourself these questions:

1.   How many hours a week am I willing to work?

2.   What time of day would be best?

3. Do I need to be home before or after school?

4. Do I need flexible time in the middle of the day?

5. Do I need to work a set schedule or is flex-time okay?

6. Do I want to work conventional workdays (Monday through Friday) or weekends?

Commitment

Some jobs want you to "sign on" for a specific period of time. You may have a contract or an agreement that a certain amount of time is a "probationary" period, after which you are instated as a full-time employee. In many organizations using a probationary period, your benefits won't be in full effect until the probationary period is over. The employer is trying to protect his or her investment in your training and wants to be sure you make it through the toughest part of the learning curve.

Commitment, from your side, means something a little different. How far up on your priority scale are you prepared to put your job, if it's the "right" job? A doctor must be willing to make a huge commitment: on-call every few nights, all night, answering pages in the middle of plays, school functions, and family dinners. Are you looking for a job you can "leave at the office," so when you're finished for the day you can simply turn off the lights and go home?

Different occupations, of course, require different degrees of commitment. Degree of commitment often means the difference between a "job" and a "career."

Generally, we are willing to make a commitment to something when we know it will pay us back long-term. In building a career, we invest time, effort, and even money. We take classes because we know the extra learning will make us more valuable to our employer. We agree to go to training seminars because we know we'll have a shot at management later.

If the job you're seeking is a short-term commitment—something to do while your kids are small, a second income to help you through a budget squeeze, or a specific answer to a need for something like additional insurance, outside companionship, or work experience—you might not be willing to make such a commitment. You don't want to be giving up 60 hours a week for a job you don't plan to be working at four months from now. You don't want to go in at 3:00 A.M. when the shift supervisor calls you.

Only you can decide what level of commitment you are willing to give your new job. There's no right or wrong, only what's comfortable for you and your family. The key is in thinking it through before you go to the interview. Know what you are offering before you get there.

Here are a few questions to ask when you're considering your commitment factor:

1. Where will this job fall in terms of our priority list?

2. Am I looking for a job that will become a career or am I looking for a part-time or temporary position?

3. Am I willing to continue my education to excel in this job?

Did I Tell You About the Time . . . ?

"I'm real proud of the five-car-carrier truck I drive. The kids think it's just the greatest thing. I was excited the day I got to bring it home and show it to them. My wife and kids were standing in the yard as I pulled the truck in the driveway. As they smiled and waved at me, I drove into the telephone wires and ripped them from the house. My wife stopped smiling."
—Father of two who works full-time

Flexibility

Flexibility is really an offshoot of commitment, because asking how flexible you're willing to be is really asking, "How much change are you willing to put up with?" Some families do well with changing or rotating schedules; others have trouble settling into a routine when Mom or Dad are always working different hours.

Some parents work on an as-needed basis. One mother, a substitute teacher in her local school system, says, "I only work when the kids are in school, and if I've got something else to do, I can do it."

Statistics show that 17 percent of the American workforce works hours other than traditional office hours.[6] Just under 4 percent of those workers have what they call "irregular" schedules that cannot be classified as either day, evening, night, or rotating shifts. If this type of arrangement is okay with you and your family—in some cases, it might nicely complement your spouse's work situation—know that before you go to the interview.

What about travel? Would you enjoy an occasional business trip, or would traveling put too much of a strain on your family?

Questions to ask about flexibility include these:

1. Can our family be flexible about my work schedule?

2. Do I need a job that is predictable, or can I be available on-call?

3. Am I willing to travel?

4. What does "flexibility" mean to me, and how flexible am I willing to be for the job I take?

I am willing to offer my employer:

Hours: _____

Overtime? _____

Flexible scheduling? _____

On-call? _____

Commitment: _____

_____

_____

Flexibility: _____

_____

_____

The "Ideal" Match

The whole idea behind thinking about what you want before you go looking for it is that the more you understand about what's important to you, the more likely you are to get it. And the more likely you are to know it when you see it. Hopefully, you'll also know when you've walked into the wrong place.

How many horror stories have you heard from people who have taken a job because they were afraid they couldn't find anything else? Maybe you've done it yourself. Many of us do it at least once in our working careers.

We've been weaving the picture of the ideal job. You know what your family needs. You've thought about your talents and aspirations. You've gotten an idea of what you're willing to give an employer in terms of time, commitment, and flexibility. Now, what is this ideal employer going to give you?

In Search of the Ideal Employer

Earlier, I mentioned that there are a number of ways to go about your job search. You might hear about job openings from friends or relatives. You might read about them in the paper. You might use an employment service, see something on-line, or catch an ad in an industry magazine. However you found it, you now have an interview.

Often we go into an interview—or the second, third, or fourth interview—thinking about what we have to offer, putting our best foot forward, appearing confident, capable, and sure. But you also need to think about what the company has to offer you. How will you know whether the company is one that will support your "family-is-important" lifestyle? There are a number of things you can look for (and ask about):

1. What is the average age of your employees?

2. Are there a number of young families here? How many?

3. What are your policies on sick days and personal days?

4. Do you have any alternative scheduling options, such as flex-time or job sharing?

5. Do you have any special child-care benefits, such as on-site day care, child-care subsidies (that's where the employer pays part of the child-care expense), summer programs, or back-up care?

These questions hit all the basics, and you'll probably know whether you're talking to a family-friendly employer as soon as you ask the first family-related question.

These are the things that are most important to me in an employer:

1. _____

2. _____

3. _____

4. _____

5. _____

6. _____

7. _____

8. _____

9. _____

10. _____

The Family-Friendly Workplace

How do you know whether the company you are interviewing with is one that is going to work for you and your family? In short, a family-friendly company will see that your family makes you a better candidate and not a lesser one. The person sitting opposite you in the interview will see the value in the many decisions you make in a day's time, the multitasking, organizing, and peacemaking qualities you bring to his or her team. He or she will look past the occasional trip to the orthodontist's office and the after-school phone calls in order to get the long-term benefit of an intelligent, capable, and dedicated employee. As one family-friendly employer put it,

"I knew when I interviewed Carol that I was in for a couple of years of babies being sick, deadlines getting stretched, and unexpected situations. But she was so creative and so talented, I knew that having her on board was worth all of that and more. Today, she's one of my best people. I've never regretted it for a minute."

Making a "Less-than-Ideal" Match Better

You may already have a job. Some things in that job might be great; others are less than you'd hoped for. Ask yourself the questions in this chapter as you think about your current job: Is it fitting the balance of home and work you'd hoped it would? Is there some rebalancing to be done? Don't feel as though you are stuck in the job with no hope of changing it. Things can always be changed.

A carefully thought-out conversation with your employer might help you understand his or her policies on family-related issues. It also might help clear the air if there are issues between you that need to be addressed. A great book for thinking about and then asking for what you want is *The Aladdin Factor*, by Jack Canfield and Mark Victor Hansen.[7] This book will help you identify what you're looking for, and show you how to ask for what you need in a clear, nonthreatening manner.

Summary

Your family is an asset, not a liability. The experience, dedication, and commitment you have invested in your family should be a benefit to your prospective employer, and not something you need to apologize for.

There still are employers out there who want to own the body, mind, and soul of an employee and who are threatened when an employee puts something else (like family) first. And those employers will find the employees they seek. But rest assured that there are many employers who look for the maturity, capability, commitment, and responsibility of an employee who seeks a challenging, progressive environment that fits in with his or her overall family and personal goals. Your job is to find them.

Notes

1. J. Michael Farr, *The Very Quick Job Search,* 2nd Edition (Indianapolis: JIST Works, 1996).

2. Ibid.

3. U.S. Department of Labor, *America's Top 300 Jobs* (Indianapolis: JIST Works, 1994); U.S. Department of Labor, *Occupational Outlook Handbook* (Indianapolis: JIST Works, 1994).

4. Farr, *The Very Quick Job Search.*

5. Ibid.

6. *Statistical Abstract of the United States 1995,* Table 635 (U.S. Government Printing Office, 1995).

7. Jack Canfield and Mark Victor Hansen, *The Aladdin Factor* (New York: Berkley Books, 1995).

The Child-Care Issue

Translations from the Child

"I don't know why. He just hit me."
He hit his brother.
"I didn't hit him. I just sort of pushed him."
He hit his brother.
"I didn't do anything."
He hit his brother.
"Mo-m-m-my!"
His brother hit him.
—Robert Paul Smith

Finding child care you're happy with is one of the most important factors in balancing home and office life. If you're worried about your children while you're at work, you're not able to focus on the job at hand. If you have questions about the situation, about the caregiver, about your child's safety—any level of concern, no matter how small—that's going to affect the level of concentration you can bring first to your job search and then to your job.

If you've got child-care arrangements worked out so that you, your spouse, and your children are all cared for and supported, you are free to do and be your best in the workforce. That's good for you and will translate to a happier parent and happier kids.

BEST &
WORST

Best:
"My own paycheck!"

This chapter presents the different options available in finding child care. We will look at a number of practical situations and discuss the things to consider and ask about each. My best advice, however, is this: *Trust your instincts.* Only you know whether your child will thrive best in a preschool, in a home, with grandma, or in a day-care program. We will look at several situations here so that you can get a bird's-eye view of the different options and focus in on the one that seems a close match to what your family needs and wants.

What's Out There?

Just as children come in all shapes, sizes, and colors, there are all kinds of child-care arrangements. The trick is to investigate what's possible; look around in your area and find out what's available; look even closer and see what's feasible (in other words, what fits your budget); then answer the most important question: Which caregiver will give your child the love, support, and protection she needs when you are not there to give it to her?

This section explores several of the most popular child-care options. I've divided them into the following categories: baby-sitters, home day care, day-care centers, care by a friend or neighbor, care by a relative, and self-care.

What Are Parents Using?

In preparing this book, a colleague and I interviewed many working parents who were using each of the different child-care options.[1] There were definite favorites—such as home-style day care—and other, rarer occurrences—like the latch-key kid alternative. Child-care choices are predicated, of course, on the needs of the child, which vary from age to age and situation to situation.

Specifically, we found:

 6 percent of respondents had in-home baby-sitters;

 31 percent arranged their work hours so Mom and Dad took care of the kids and no day care was needed;

 25 percent took their children to home-run day care;

 14 percent used local day-care centers;

 6 percent relied on friends or neighbors;

 14 percent took their children to other family members (aunts, grandparents, etc.);

 6 percent of the parents interviewed allowed their children to stay home alone. (All of the parents in this category had children over the age of 10, usually with at least one teenager in the home.)[2]

Figure 3.1 shows the results of these informal interviews.

How Our Parents Responded

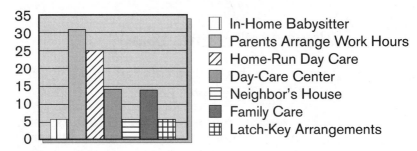

☐ In-Home Babysitter
■ Parents Arrange Work Hours
▨ Home-Run Day Care
■ Day-Care Center
☰ Neighbor's House
■ Family Care
▦ Latch-Key Arrangements

Figure 3.1

Things to Consider

Many parents prefer to work out child-care arrangements themselves, so their children spend a minimum of time in someone else's care. A fairly high number of respondents—26 percent— said that they have arranged their work schedules so Mom has the kids when Dad is working and vice versa.

Home-run day care was the second most popular choice, showing up as the child-care solution for 25 percent of those interviewed.

Grandma or Grandpa is the logical next choice, with 14 percent relying on family members to fill in the gaps of child care. Another 6 percent had their children stay with neighbors until they were able to get home from work.

As you think about the type of child care that will work for you, several factors will weigh heavily:

 The ages of your children and the care they need

 The hours (both the number and the range of hours) you need child care

 the cost of different kinds of child care

Your Child's Age

It's no secret that children need care; and they need loving care no matter what age they are. Different ages bring different responsibilities, however. An infant needs one kind of care; a ninth-grader needs another.

Some parents arrange to work swing shifts so they can keep their child at home while he is an infant and then make day-care or preschool arrangements when he is old enough to want socialization. One mother puts it this way:

◆ ◆

"From the time Sara was born until she was 18 months old, my employer allowed me to work at home three days a week. Then, all of a sudden, when Sara turned one-and-a-half, Mom wasn't interesting anymore. She was ready to be social, and I began taking her to day care and went back to work at the office full-time. Things are great—we enjoy being together more than ever now that we're each doing our own thing."
—Mother of one who works full-time

◆ ◆

Your Hours

All working parents try set up the best possible child care for their child. For some, that means a little of this and a little of that. Your daughter might go to the baby-sitter's on Tuesday and Thursday and to preschool on Monday, Wednesday, and Friday mornings. Perhaps you are able to work at home those three afternoons, or she goes to a neighbor's house and you pick her up on your way home.

When you are thinking about the type of child care you need, think about the hours you'll be needing it. If you are just beginning to look for a job, you don't know the actual hours you will be working, but you will have an idea of what you're *willing* to work, which you can use as a guideline for the hours you'll need child care.

If your second-grader only needs someone to watch him from 3:00 P.M., when he gets off the bus, until 5:10, when you get home, you might be able to work it out with a neighbor for those couple of after-school hours a day. If you've got a toddler who needs full-time child care, you'll probably be looking for a home-run day care, a day-care center, a relative, or some kind of swing shift arrangement with your spouse. Remember that the key is to come up with the schedule and practical arrangements to support what is important to your family. So what if you do something different every day of the week, as long as everyone is okay with it? Or perhaps you will go the other way and keep a very regimented schedule. That's okay, too. The idea is to come up with a system that works for you and provides the best possible care for your children.

Your Budget

None of us would choose a particular kind of child care—especially if we thought it was substandard— simply because of the cost. More likely, if we are faced with child-care costs that are too high and the need to work, we will scramble like crazy to come up with as many options as we can find.

But different kinds of child care are going to cost differing amounts. Nannies—private, in-home caregivers acquired through a service—cost upwards of $200 a week. An in-home baby-sitter might charge half that, although other services, such as laundry or dishes, might be extra. In-home day care might range from $45 to $100 a week (maybe higher in some areas), and day-care centers offer a range of hours and choices that also put you in the $100 and up bracket. If you add another child, you're looking at $150+ a week in child-care expenses alone, which adds up quickly week after week after week.

Many businesses today are willing to help parents by subsidizing the cost of day care. Talk to local day-care providers to see which businesses in your area participate in subsidized programs. And don't forget to ask about day-care subsidies as a benefit in your job interviews!

There is an option—or a combination of options—that will work for you. Keep looking until you find it. And once you make your child-care decisions, make it a point to reevaluate every so often. Nothing is set in stone, and the key to making things better is being able to look at them and ask yourself (and your kids) how everything is working out.

What Kind of Care Do We Need?

List each child's name and age and the type of care he or she needs; for example,

Brandon, 8, after-school care

Emily, 2, all day

How much can we afford to spend on child care?

Child-Care Options

Once you've established that you'll need to rely on someone other than yourself, your spouse, or your family for at least part of the time, you have a number of avenues to consider. You might want to allow your children to stay at home and have the caregiver come to them. You might take them to another person's home. Or you might enroll them in a day-care center. This section discusses those different options and gives you checklists for evaluating each.

In-Home Sitter

It may be every working parent's dream: your very own Mrs. Doubtfire, perhaps retired after many years of teaching school, searching for a special child she can love and care for and bake chocolate-chip cookies with. She comes to your home, she does the laundry and the dishes, she takes wonderful care of your kids, gets them to their appointments, lessons, and friend's houses on time, and starts dinner for you on the days you're running late.

The in-home sitter is a wonderful option provided (1) you can find just the right person and (2) you can afford her. Many in-home sitters do become members of the family, often taking on other household responsibilities in addition to caring for the children. One mother who has successfully worked with an in-home sitter for years has this tip to offer:

"Make your sitter a part of your family. Treat her with respect, and never take advantage of her! There is mutual love between my children and our sitter, and I'm glad."
—Mother of two who works full-time

Where can you find an in-home sitter? The answer depends on the type of sitter you're hoping for. Nannies, once a luxury, are now becoming more commonplace in the two-career family. You can contact an agency to interview a range of potential nannies and hire the one that best fits your household. How much will you pay for a nanny? That varies greatly, depending on the area you live in. But, generally, you should expect to pay a premium—$200 to $300 a week and higher—for premium, customized child care.

If you want to find an in-home sitter in a more informal undertaking, think about what type of sitter you're looking for. Your church is a good place to start. Other places to try include a local university (often they have a referral service for students looking for placements; someone majoring in education would be a logical choice as a sitter). Perhaps the most often-used source for good in-home care is the advice of friends and neighbors. Maybe your friend had a sitter who was wonderful last summer but won't be needing her services this summer. Keep your eyes and ears open and the right in-home sitter may come to you.

What are some things to look for in a good in-home sitter? Here is a list of considerations[3]:

 How interested is she in your child?

 How does she interact with the child? Is she listening attentively or focusing on other things?

 Does she seem to be creative?

 What does she think is the most important thing about caring for a child?

 Does your child seem to like her?

 Is she willing to drive to appointments or carpool if necessary?

 Will she do any other household chores?

Before you hire an in-home sitter, invite her over to "play" at least twice in an informal setting. Let her interact with your children and give them a chance to get comfortable together, with you nearby.

Make sure, when you find the sitter who will work for your family, that you discuss how to resolve any issues that might arise. Talk about discipline, stresses, financial situations, and illness. Iron out the wrinkles up-front, as much as possible.

Remember, too, that an employee you have in your home is an employee nonetheless. Check with your accountant and make sure you've got the right paperwork filed with the IRS.

Questions to Ask

1. What is your background? _____
   _____

2. What do you enjoy most about working with kids?
   _____

3. What's hardest for you in caring for children? ____
   _____

4. Describe the last situation in which you cared for kids.
   Why did you leave? _____
   _____

5. _____
6. _____
7. _____
8. _____
9. _____
10. _____

The most important word of advice about hiring an in-home sitter is this: Get references and check them. It is possible to do this without affronting or insulting the prospective caregiver. Anyone who loves children will understand your need to be thorough in making sure you've hired the best possible person to care for your child.

Home Day Care

The second largest percentage of working parents we interviewed (25 percent) take their children to home-run day cares. This situation often is one in which the caregiver, usually a mother herself, takes four to ten children into her home on a full-time or part-time basis.

Home day care is done on a formal, accredited or an informal basis. Many cities have agencies that can give you the names, locations, and phone numbers of accredited home day cares in your area. An accredited home day-care center will follow guidelines determined by the agency, which usually keeps tabs on the number of children in the home, the ages of the children, the adult-to-children ratio, and meal plans. Additionally, the agency may provide information to caregivers on topics such as the importance of immunizations, planning healthy snacks, and how to reduce germs and colds with safe household products.

From One Parent to Another
"When you're looking at home day cares or day-care centers, don't take your child to every one you visit. Take him only to the two or three best. That will let him be part of the decision without overwhelming him with the ones you don't like."
—Mother of two who works full-time

How do you find a home-run day care? Start by looking for a child-care agency in your area. Look in the *Yellow Pages* under Child Care or even Preschools. You also may want to contact your local Child and Family Services division (a segment of your local government) to find out what agencies and services are available.

Friends and family are a good source of information on home-run day care, as are other parents at work or the parents of children in your child's class at school.

Once you've found a home-run day care you want to check out, go and visit by yourself first. Observe and ask about the following things:

 Is the overall atmosphere of the home happy or harried?

 Is there a separate "child area" with easels, tables and chairs, toys, and/or blocks where the children feel welcome to play with abandon?

 Does the day-care provider offer a set schedule during which she does different activities with the children?

 How does she handle nap time?

 What does she do when she has one or more sick children at home?

 How is discipline handled?

 Is there an outdoor, fenced play area with play equipment appropriate to the ages of the children?

Again, ask for references. The day-care provider can probably give you the names and numbers of the parents of some of her other charges. When you get the numbers, make the calls. The provider won't mind you checking, and the parents won't mind giving their input. Everyone understands the need to make sure one's children are protected and cared for.

Home Safe Home

One of the biggest differences between a day-care center and a home-run day care—besides the number of children—is the adherence to health and safety guidelines. In order to be licensed, day-care centers must meet with strict state requirements. If you are electing to use a home-run day care, you'll need to think about and ask about some safety issues yourself.

- Does the day-care provider have an adequate number of fire alarms and extinguishers?

- Does she have an exit plan that she explains to the children about where to go and what to do in case of fire?

- Does she teach the children how to call 911?

- Where do they go in case of inclement weather?

These are not issues that need to be resolved on your first visit, but they are important things to address before you begin dropping your child off in the morning.

The Day-Care Center

A smaller percentage (14 percent) of the parents we interviewed used day-care centers. But nationwide, day-care centers provide a massive amount of support to parents in a variety of occupations with a wide range of working hours. A day-care center typically cares for a large number of children, ranging in ages from 6 weeks to 12 years. (Not all day-care centers are licensed for infant care. Check the centers in your area to see which ones provide the services you need.)

A typical day in a day-care center is similar to that of a preschool, only longer. Your child will probably have circle time, story time, drawing and coloring, puzzle time, snack time, lunch time, nap time, music, and other activities. Some day-care centers focus strongly on academics and offer things like computer time (even for 2- and 3-year-olds), field trips, and Montessori-style lessons.

The Montessori method of teaching, designed by Sister Maria Montessori in the early 1900s, focuses on experiential learning. Children learn about measuring by spooning rice into a cup; they learn their letters by tracing the outline of the letter on a sandpaper block; they get the basics of mathematical operations by working with blocks and beads. This enables even pre-readers to grasp many of the basic concepts they'll learn later, all in fun, nonthreatening activities.

Many day-care centers offer activities or low-key learning experiences that are based on the Montessori method. Ask your day-care center how they handle academic issues. Experts agree that the primary focus for preschoolers should be on fun and socialization. They'll have plenty of time for academics later.

A good day-care center, like a happy home-run day-care situation, can be a terrific experience for your children. They might love the interaction; they might enjoy the stimulation; and many children of working parents like having their own "work" to go to.

The hours of day-care centers usually are limited, however, and parents who work nontraditional hours are often left to find other child care. There is a need today for 24-hour day-care centers, where children can spend the night if their parents work the graveyard shift; for weekend care, for parents in nontraditional occupations like retail or other service businesses; and for sick-child care, for the child "on the mend," not seriously ill but not recovered enough for school. These options are available, but not widely so. Their numbers are still small.

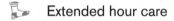

Parents' Wish Lists

The following items are on parents' wish lists for day care. The need is there, but the services are slow in coming:

 Extended hour care

 Weekend care

 24-hour care

Drop-in care

 Overnight care

Sick-child care

Here are a few questions you will want to ask the director of the day-care center when you visit:

What is the overall mission statement of the day-care center?

Has a formal complaint of any kind ever been filed against the day-care center? If so, what was the situation and how was it resolved? If not, what should a parent do if he or she has a question or concern?

How accessible is the director of the center? What is the director's background, and what does she or he find most challenging about running the center successfully?

How does enrollment at the center compare to the enrollment a year ago? Is the enrollment growing? Have the necessary number of teachers and aides been added?

The following sections break down by age groups the things you might want to consider as you're looking for a day-care center for your child. Bear in mind that many of the issues will apply to any child-care arrangements you make, not only day-care centers. The key is to go in knowing what you're looking for; then you'll know it when you do (or don't) find it.

Infants and Toddlers

Babies need laps to sit on and hands to hold. One of the most important things for an infant or toddler in day care is that there be an adequate number of adults to care for the children present. Most states have strict requirements about the adult-to-child ratio, particularly where infants and toddlers are concerned. Check the requirement for your state, and make sure that any caregiver you investigate adheres strictly to state guidelines.

Here's a quick list of things to look for:

 Is the center a happy place? Is the atmosphere laughing and loving or tense and quiet?

 What kind of training does the staff participate in?

 Is there a nurse on-staff?

 How long have the infant and toddler teachers been with the staff? Children will bond with their caregivers, and a frequent turnover in teachers could be unsettling to your child. It also could be an indication that something is wrong with the management of the center.

 Are there plenty of cribs?

Is there a comfortable play area, with a rug for on-the-floor play?

How many rocking chairs are in the room?

Does the center have outdoor playground equipment suitable for small children?

Is there a separate fenced play area apart from the older children's playground?

Is the diaper changing area clean and odor-free?

Ask to see any toys your child will be playing with. How do the teachers deter the spread of germs with the bunch of "chewers" they have in class every day?

Questions for Later

1. What items from home will you need to provide for your baby? _____

_____

2. How many diapers does the center need on-hand?

_____

3. What about bottles and pacifiers?

_____

4. How does the center handle it when your child is on a prescription? _____

_____

5. _____
6. _____
7. _____
8. _____
9. _____
10. _____

Preschoolers

If you're considering a day-care center for your preschooler, you'll have a different set of concerns on your checklist. The same safety and cleanliness issues apply, but there will be other things to watch for, as well.

 What is the class size? How many adults are available for your child's class? There may be one full-time teacher and a teacher's aide, depending on the age group and the number of children in the class.

 Are there child-sized tables and chairs? Most centers also have child-sized toilet facilities and are equipped for both small and middle-sized (school-aged) children.

 What does the staff do in the event of scrapes and bruises? At what point do they notify you? Is there an accident report form or some reporting policy they follow in case of an injury?

 What types of meals are offered? Licensed day-care centers must follow state guidelines for nutrition; these guidelines require that lunch menus be posted weekly, so parents can see what their children are eating during the day.

 What happens during a typical day? Is there a balance between action and quiet times? How many times a day will your child be read to? Will he or she get to play on the playground? What happens on rainy or cold days?

 What does the general learning atmosphere feel like? At preschool age, learning should be an exploration: you should see plenty of toys for "pretend"—dress-up clothes, toy kitchens, blocks. While preschoolers are apt to learn things like colors, shapes, numbers, and maybe letters, there shouldn't be any pressure on them to learn at this age. Preschool should be fun.

 How is discipline handled? If you don't see any signs of it going on around you, ask. Day-care centers usually use a "time-out" method to discipline. Get clear guidance on what's acceptable behavior and what is not.

Questions for Later

1. Does your preschooler need a change of clothes to keep at the center?

2. Are blankets and stuffed animals okay for naptime?

3. What is the policy for bringing favorite toys from home?

4. _____

5. _____

6. _____

7. _____

8. _____

9. _____

10. _____

The School-Aged Child

Most day-care centers have some kind of after-school club or activity center for school-aged children. Some also offer transportation to and from area schools and provide field trips and other incentives— such as computer time—for older children.

When you're investigating a day-care center for your school-aged child, make sure you visit during the time the school-agers are in the building. See how the teacher (or teachers) handle the kids. Are the children kept busy? Are they working with age-appropriate materials, or are they using toys and building sets meant for younger children? Are there plenty of children in your child's age group, or is he one of the oldest or youngest? Sociability is an important factor in both what your child learns and how well he adjusts to his environment.

Many day-care centers have more school-agers enrolled during the summer and school vacations over the holidays. And many of these centers use field trips to keep the children busy. If you're okay with your child going to the museum on Monday, the zoo on Tuesday, the pool on Wednesday and Friday, and perhaps a picnic on Thursday, you may find a day-care center is just what you want for your school-aged child. If your kids are like mine, however, they want to spend the first month of summer vacation sitting around in their pajamas until noon, when they start thinking about who they can get to take them to the pool. (Hey, if I could get away with sitting around in my robe watching cartoons until noon every day, I'd do it, too!) Check with the day-care center to see if your kids will be allowed any unstructured time, time they can spend reading, relaxing, or watching cartoons.

Another important issue to explore if you're thinking about a day-care center for your school-aged child is what they do about discipline. Dealing with 10 or 12 jeering fourth graders is no small feat. How do the teachers handle it? Again, get very clear directions on what's acceptable and what's not, and—before you enroll her—go over the list with your child. Make sure you both know what you're walking into.

Questions for Later

1. Do you pick up after school?

2. If my child participates in sports, can you provide transportation to the center after practice?

3. Do you have any club activities, such as scouting or 4-H, available for school-agers at the center?

4. _____

5. _____

6. _____

7. _____

8. _____

9. _____

10. _____

Workplace Child Care

A decade ago, finding a day-care center in or around an office was nearly unheard of. Today, some large corporations have a day care on premises; others make arrangements with nearby centers to help offset child-care costs for employees or in other ways subsidize child care.

BEST &
WORST

Worst:
"Making
arrangements
when
kids are
off school"

In return for their family-friendly investment, these employers enjoy many benefits, including happier employees, less turnover, and higher productivity. Parents can easily have lunch with their children, be close by in case of bumps and bruises, and work with peace of mind knowing their children are nearby.

If the job you are investigating does not offer any kind of child care or subsidies (which means they pay for a portion of the care and you have a reduced fee because you are a member of the organization), you can always try to get something started later. Chapter 9 explores the different avenues you can follow to make family issues more prevalent in your organization or office.

What Kind of Child Care Is Best for Us?

First Choice: _____

Second Choice: _____

Third Choice: _____

Alternatives/Comments: _____

_____

_____

_____

The Latch-Key Alternative

So you have successfully made it through the baby-sitter and day-care stages. Now you are facing the home-alone stage. Your 12-year-old doesn't want to go to the sitter's house this summer. She's old enough to stay home on her own, she insists. You consider. Is she? What about phone calls, and cooking, and strangers at the door?

It's a big decision. The "ideal" latch-key situation (if there is one) is the one where your 16-year-old is home to watch the 12-year-old during the summer. Yes, they are both kids, but a 16-year-old is better equipped than a 12-year-old to deal with the decisions that come up during the day.

Most parents who rely on latch-key situations insist their children follow a regimented schedule: "As soon as you get off the bus, go right into the house and call me to let me know you're home. Get yourself a snack (I put one in the fridge for you), and get busy on your homework. You can watch TV or play video games until I get home at 5:00. But no friends in, and you can't go out until I get home."

Doesn't sound like a lot of fun. But with proper guidelines, your child will be safe, be proud of taking care of herself, and be able to get homework at least started (with some peripheral dawdling) before you get home.

 If you let your child stay home alone, make sure you post the phone number of a close relative or friend who can help out in any situation: when your child is frightened, can't get a jar open, has a homework question, or just wants to talk. And of course post emergency numbers and make sure your child knows what to do in case of bad weather or other unexpected happenings.

Did I Tell You About the Time . . . ?

"When our children were first old enough to stay home by themselves, I told them to tell people who called that I was in the shower and couldn't come to the phone. The only problem is that if the caller then asks for my husband, the kids say 'He's in the shower, too!'"
—Mother of two who works part-time

Rules for Staying Home Alone

1. _____
2. _____
3. _____
4. _____
5. _____
6. _____
7. _____

Emergency Numbers:

Police: _____

Fire: _____

Mom at work: _____

Dad at work: _____

Neighbor: _____

Making Day Care Work

Once you get the job, find the child care, and begin moving into a regular routine, what can you do to keep things running smoothly? Here are a few tips that will help you anticipate and maybe bypass problems with your caregiver.

Establish your schedule, and stick to it. Don't vary
your drop-off time every day and—especially after
a long, harried day—call if you're going to be more
than 15 minutes late.

When you think your schedule will change—say
you're covering another worker's hours for a two-
week period—let your caregiver know as soon as
possible. This will enable her to make necessary
arrangements to accommodate the change.

If you have a flexible work schedule, give your
caregiver a copy of your schedule as soon as you
have it. Telling her is okay, but having it in writing
lets her refer to it later.

If "drop-ins" are okay with your caregiver and it's
possible you might need her services on a stray
day here and there, talk to her about it first. Call
and ask whether it's okay, preferably a week or so
in advance. This helps you know how many
children she'll have so you can plan activities for
the day.

When you have questions or concerns, express
them in a respectful, caring way. If you're upset
because Janie said one of the babies bit her, don't
call the caregiver up and read her the riot act.
When you drop Janie off in the morning, explain
what Janie told you and ask the caregiver if she is
having a problem with one of the babies biting.
Talk about the situation constructively: What's
being tried? How can you help? What can you tell
Janie to do if it happens again? Look at how you
can help the situation, and fight the impulse to
explode. (And if your child has been hurt, that
impulse is probably there.) Remember that the
relationship you establish with your child's
caregiver is an important one both for your child
and for you, and preserving it with open
communication and respect is vital to keeping it
healthy.

Ask the caregiver questions to show you're
interested in her day. Asking "How are things

going?" or "Is there anything you need me to bring?" lets the caregiver know you are interested in how things are working out and are open to hearing about any ways you can improve the situation.

Basic friendliness and appreciation go a long way. Gifts on holidays, thank-you notes, and little expressions of concern and caring for a special caregiver cement her place in your lives as an important part of your family system.

Summary

Sorting through child-care options can be overwhelming: There are a number of options out there, and each is worthy of careful consideration. With your family priorities and mission statement in hand, you should be able to identify the types of child care that are most appropriate for your family. Once you've identified the types of care you'll consider, think about things like the hours you need child care, the age of your children, and the amount of money you can spend.

Being a proactive parent means getting educated and taking steps toward getting what you want for your family. In finding the right care for your children, you ensure a happier balance for everyone and a better working mindset for yourself.

Notes

1. The following percentages are based on inter-
    views a colleague and I conducted in our local
    area with 65 working parents. Numbers may
    be different in your area, depending on
    whether you live in a rural or urban setting
    and the population size and make-up of the
    workforce in your area.

2. Eleven percent of interview respondents did
    not answer the child-care question.

3. Please note that, although I use the pronoun
    "she" to refer to your potential sitter, I don't
    mean to discount the possibility of a "he." Both
    men and women can make good sitters. The
    "she" simply recognizes that the vast majority
    of child-care providers are women.

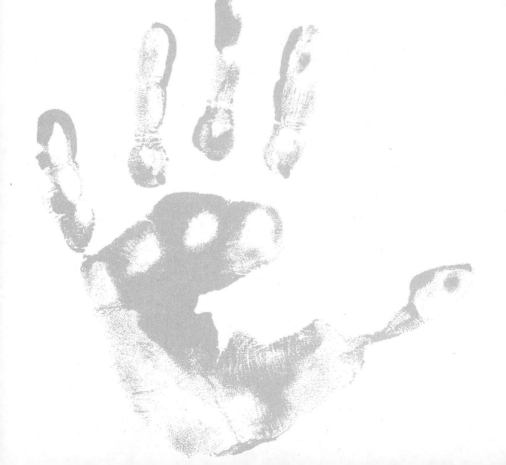

Chapter

4

"Your Sitter Is on Line 1"

*"Big sisters are the crabgrass
in the lawn of life."*
–Charles M. Schultz

Receptionists in large corporations will be the
first to tell you: 3:30 is a busy time at the
switchboard. Calls come in, calls go out. Moms
and dads want to know the kids have made it
home safe. Kids want to know what they can
have for a snack—and is it okay if they play
soccer at Todd's?

As a working parent, don't expect one nice, neat little phone call a day. That may be what you hope for, and that may be what you eventually settle into, but at first you're likely to get several calls a day if your child is at a baby-sitter's or grandma's; fewer—perhaps none—if your child is in a day-care center or at school.

How many phone calls are too many, and how do employers feel about it? Employers know that the parents on their staffs need to check in at home in order to feel comfortable that their children are being well cared for. A parent preoccupied with a child's safety is not going to be a productive employee. Understanding this, most employers won't begrudge you phone contact, although asking about and then adhering to any company policy on personal calls is a smart move. Show your boss that you respect the system, but maintain that your family responsibilities are a priority.

Limit your phone contact to a time that's convenient—for you and for others in your area who are reliant on either the phone or your attention—and then stick to it.

Schedule a time with your child to connect during the day. You might leave it as, "Call me as soon as you get home," or, "Call me right after 'Animaniacs,'" but make sure that your child knows that calling every 5 or 10 minutes is going to be hazardous to both your sanity and your job. If you've got two children at home together—either with a sitter or alone—you might be barraged early on with "he-said/she-said" phone calls, in which each one calls to tell on the other. Set your rules clearly about this kind of behavior and establish what you will and will not accept as a legitimate excuse for a phone call.

If you don't have the opportunity to talk to your child during the day, you can share a thought instead. I went back to work the same year my daughter started full-day kindergarten. We'd always been together and it was hard on both of us to separate so completely and so suddenly. We agreed to think of each other every day at 11:00 A.M.; and then each night, one of us would invariably ask, "Did you think of me today?" It helped us make the transition and reminded us that even when we're apart, we're not really apart.

Here are a couple of tips for organizing the phone-in, phone-out aspect of your working life:

 Establish a contact time. If you have kids home alone, or kids getting off the bus at a baby-sitter's house, designate a time for them to call you or for you to call them. Make it a quick, pleasant call—not one of those "I-told-you-to-take-out-the-trash-this-morning-and-you-didn't-do-it" calls—and find out how the day went, what homework they've got to do, and so on. A five-minute call that says "I just wanted to make sure you're safe and let you know I love you" is all that's really necessary to set both you and your children at ease.

 Define "callable" events. If your children go to the house of a sitter, friend, or relative during the day, make sure you outline clearly in what situations you do—or do not—want to be called. Do you want your sitter to call and ask you whether Heidi can have a chocolate bunny before lunch? Is a sore throat a problem, or is it okay for you to find out about that at the end of the day? If Tommy swallows a penny, do you want the sitter to call you before or after she picks him up by his feet to see if it falls out on its own? Think about a number of situations—your sitter or other caregiver can help you—and determine whether you think each a callable offense. Make a list for your caregiver—with your work number at the top—so she'll know when and how to call you. Something like this would do the trick:

Call me at 375-5555

1. If Trina begins running a fever.

2. If she gets hurt and is upset for more than five minutes without calming down or being distracted by something else.

3. In any emergency situation; illness, injury, household accidents, etc.

Depending on where you are taking your child for child care, you may want to be notified before any excursions. For example, if you take your daughter to a baby-sitter's house and the sitter doesn't usually take the children anywhere during the day, you might ask to be notified before she takes your child to the park for the afternoon. On the other hand, if field trips are a part of your arrangement—as would be the case with a day-care center—there's no need for the call.

All parents, of course, need to know their children are safe. We need check-in points. We need to know our children and their caregivers have access to us whenever they need us. The trick is to think about and define what you consider a "necessary" phone call. This will keep you from tying up the lines and let you be more productive at work.

These are the best times to contact me in nonemergency situations:

1. _____
2. _____
3. _____

Take Two Aspirins and I'll See You in the Morning

Another home issue that will affect you at work is the health of your children. We've already established that times of change bring on reduced immune systems. Combine that with the germ-ripe environment of a day-care center and, presto—you've got a sick child.

Statistics show that, on average, a working parent misses 1 day every 12 weeks because a child is sick. Bradley misses school, you miss work. It's that simple.

In some areas, sick-child care is available. In these centers, nurses help care for children who are not contagious or seriously ill, those on the mend who are not well enough to be at school. There are plenty of critics of sick-child programs, those who say that a sick child should be at home with a parent, no matter what. But there are just as many working parents who truly need this kind of service in order to continue providing for their families.

Another interesting statistic shows, not surprisingly, that more mothers than fathers stay home with sick children, and that mothers of children under 6 miss more days than do mothers of school-aged children.[1]

What should you do when your child gets sick? Let's break this into two parts: Consider your options, and then decide what you want to do. This is one of those discussions you'll want to have with your spouse or partner, so you can both share in the child-care hospice responsibilities.

Sick-Care Options

When Celia gets sick and needs to stay home from school, what are your options?

The first response to this question is another question: How sick is she? If she's running a fever and throwing up, she needs to be home in bed, not at a sitter's exposing other children or at Grandma's, giving her the flu. If she's got something not infectious, like an ear infection, and feels comfortable drinking juice and watching movies on Grandma's couch, Grandma's house might be an option.

Next, consider what resources are available in your area for child care. If Celia is well enough to go somewhere, where can she go? Do you have a friend or neighbor who could watch her while you get in a few hour's work? Is your mother or father available? Can your spouse come home for a few hours so you can work tag-team style?

Are there partial alternatives you're not considering? In this age of connectivity, can you work at home on your computer and transfer files to the office? Can you run in and get the work you need, then work at home for the afternoon?

Is there a day-care center near your workplace—or perhaps in your workplace—that offers sick-child care? In many larger cities, these options are becoming more and more available.

There may be all sorts of options in your area. The best idea is to check them out and decide what you want before you need them.

These people can watch the kids if they are sick but not contagious:

First Choice

Name: _____

Phone: _____

Second Choice

Name: _____

Phone: _____

Third Choice

Name: _____

Phone: _____

Creating a Sick-Day Plan

Now that you know what your options are, sit down with your spouse or partner and map out a plan of action for that first day you are awakened at 4:30 A.M. by, "Mommy, I'm sick."

BEST & WORST

Best: "I can't *wait* to see my kids at the end of the day!"

If both you and your spouse have equal work arrangements (meaning it's equally inconvenient for both of you to take off for a nonsick sick day), you might agree to swap days. If Michael is home from school both Monday and Tuesday, for example, you take Monday off and your spouse handles Tuesday (or vice versa).

If neither of you can comfortably take off an entire day, you might try alternating mornings and afternoons. Sometimes it's easier to get off early or late than it is to miss a whole 8-hour day.

Again, take the time to think about what you want before you need it. Write it down and post it on your information center. Explain to the kids what will happen on sick days before they get sick. Don't tell Trina as you're wrapping her in a blanket and putting her in the van, "You're going to stay at Grandma's while I go in to work for a few hours." A sick child being shuttled here and there is more likely to resist than a well child being shuttled here and there. Have a plan made so, when the sick days come—and they will—all you have to do is follow your prescribed plan.

Sick-Day Plan

If one of the children gets sick during the day, this is how we will handle it:

First Choice

_____

_____

_____

_____

Second Choice

_____

_____

_____

_____

Third Choice

_____

_____

_____

_____

Remember, too, that not all sick days are full-day events. How will you handle it when the school calls and tells you your child is running a fever and needs to go home? Sometimes, this can actually be a blessing—you've been at work for a few hours so you don't feel as guilty as you might missing a whole day's work, and you have the opportunity to grab work to take home.

Will you be the one responsible for picking up your child from school if the nurse calls? Will your spouse do it? What about the baby-sitter or a neighbor? If it's possible that you might not be available, make sure you have a back-up plan in case you can't be reached.

All schools require emergency numbers of friends or relatives they can call when they can't reach you. Make sure you've informed those people—whether it's your mother, your friend, or your sitter—that if the school can't reach you when your child is sick, they are next on the list.

Handling Emergencies

Emergencies come in all shapes and sizes. An emergency might be that Wendy wet her pants and doesn't have any dry ones at day care. Josh falling and breaking his arm on the playground is definitely an emergency.

What kind of emergencies you'll have and how you will respond (and how smoothly you will respond) will depend on your situation. Everyone has them, but we can lessen their likelihood by keeping these factors in mind:

 Accidents happen more often when children are tired or hungry. You've probably noticed the tendency in yourself to be less alert when your resources are depleted. Your children experience the same thing, although they probably won't admit it. They might miss that last step, trip over the toy truck, or just run into something that wasn't there a moment ago.

 Accidents occur more frequently in a new place. If you have just started day care, are visiting at a relative's house, or have recently moved, watch for a higher number of accidents while your child gets used to the new surroundings.

Accidents are more likely if you've recently changed your child's schedule. If you've just returned to work and started dropping your child off at day care or a baby-sitter's house, you've definitely modified your schedule. Watch for increased clumsiness and take a few common-sense precautions to make accidents less likely.

Common-Sense Safety Tips

A little common sense can help you reduce accidents during this transitional time:

 Tie your child's shoes in double-knots so he doesn't trip over the laces

 Dress your child in loose-fitting clothes that she can move freely in.

 If you pack a lunch for your preschooler or toddler, omit anything that is a potential choking hazard: raw carrots in your 3-year-old's lunch when you're not there to watch him is risky: He might be so busy talking to the other kids at his table that he doesn't pay attention to the big chunks he's swallowing.

 Check any toys your child wants to take to day care: Something that is perfectly fine at home can present a problem at school if it has rough edges or a pointed antenna.

 Make sure your child has "action shoes"— shoes made for running, jumping, and climbing. Dressing up is great, and so are dress-up shoes. But if they are slick on the bottom, they will slide on the center's linoleum floors and greatly increase the likelihood that your child will wipe out on a hurried trip to the rest room.

 Make sure your child's clothes are appropriate for the season. Many of us have

been up against the will of a fashion-conscious 4-year-old: It's 30 degrees outside and she's determined to wear her pink sundress and sandals. Remember that she's more likely to have an accident if she's too cold, too warm, too tired, or overstimulated. (That pretty well covers the entire day of a 4-year-old, doesn't it?)

What Is an Emergency?

Webster's defines an emergency as "an unforeseen combination of circumstances or the resulting state that calls for immediate action." That seems to sum it up. In the last section, we discussed some ways you can cut down on the number of "unforeseen circumstances" that might contribute to an emergency. In this section, you'll develop a plan so you can handle the "resulting state that calls for immediate action."

Developing an Emergency Plan

First, define what constitutes an emergency in your family. Is a forgotten lunch an emergency? What about a missed school bus? The big ones you won't need to define: sprained ankles, injuries requiring stitches, or a sudden severe illness that needs Mom's or Dad's attention. It's the little ones you need to determine how you're going to handle. What is an emergency in your family? Toss it out on the table at the family meeting and come up with your own definition.

In our family, these are emergencies:

1. _____

2. _____

3. _____

4. _____

5. _____

Next, consider what actions you will take in an emergency situation. If possible, come up with one procedure you can use for all emergencies. Coming up with the answers to these questions will help you devise your plan:

1. In case of an emergency, do you want the school or day care to call you or your spouse first? The answer to this question is not about who cares the most but, rather, who can get there fastest. If you work on an assembly line and have to call for someone to replace you, you might have a longer wait than a person who can drop everything and go.

2. Who will you use as a back-up if you are unreachable? Is there a neighbor, friend, or relative who will agree to be an emergency stand-in if you can't be reached right away?

3. What hospital is nearest to your child's school, day-care center, or baby-sitter's house?

4. Do both you and your spouse (and any caregiver who might be responsible for taking a child to the emergency room) have current insurance numbers and permissions?

See "All-Important Permissions" below for information on how give your caregiver written permission to get medical help for your child in case of an emergency.

5. If you are called away to handle an emergency, what will happen to your other children? If you usually pick them up at school, you'll need a back-up plan. Make sure the kids know beforehand—that's part of the plan—who will be picking them up if something out of the ordinary happens. Stress that your absence or the change in routine does not necessarily mean that something horrible has happened—it might mean only that you were kept late in a meeting or had a late appointment. We want our children to be prepared—but not panicked—when they experience a change in the routine.

Code Words

Many families use a code word to signal a child that the adult providing the back-up care was really sent by the parent. In an ideal situation, your mother, your spouse, or your best friend will pick up your children from school when you can't. But if someone outside your normal support group needs to pick up the kids, make sure they know the family code word. Teach your children that it's okay—expected, even—for them to ask the adult what the code word is. If the adult doesn't know the word or forgets it, the children don't go with him or her. It's as simple as that.

Recently in our area, an 8-year-old boy saved himself from abduction at a city park using this very technique. A stranger approached and told the boy his mother wanted him and that she was on the other side of the park. The stranger offered to take the boy to his mother. The boy asked what the code word was. When the man didn't know, the boy threw his bookbag at him and ran in the opposite direction, yelling for the police. The man was apprehended as he tried to leave the park, and the boy made the nightly news two nights in a row, a symbol of smart family protection in the '90s.

Posting Emergency Procedures

Once you come up with the answers to your emergency questions, put them together in a plan that can be easily understood and followed by family members. If you have a child who changes locations during the day—for example, Jimmy is at school from 8:00 to 3:00, then home alone from 3:00 to 5:00—you need two emergency procedures: one for what happens if the school calls with an emergency and one for what happens if Jimmy calls from home in an emergency situation. In the second case, Jimmy needs a set of procedures he can follow until you get home or help arrives. We'll tackle each of these issues separately.

The Family Emergency Procedure

Make sure you've got all the following items included on a family emergency procedure:

 Important phone numbers: Police, fire, poison control center, Mom's work, Dad's work, the closest neighbor or friend.

 Step-by-step listing of what will happen in an emergency. Include an explanation of how each child's schedule will change in an emergency situation. The following list presents an idea of how you could break down the different steps:

1. If Aaron has an emergency at school, the school knows to call me at work. If Elizabeth has an emergency at Linda's house, Linda will call me at work.

2. I will quickly call Dad and tell him what's going on.

3. I will leave work immediately and go get Aaron or Elizabeth.

4. If the situation involves Aaron, Dad will notify Elizabeth's sitter that he will be picking her up at 5:45 instead of me picking her up at 3:30. He will talk to Elizabeth and explain what's happening. If the situation involves Elizabeth, Dad will leave work and pick up Aaron at 3:15 in front of the school building and take him back to the office with him until 5:30.

5. If it is a medical emergency, we will go to Riverview Hospital. If it is not a medical emergency, I will take Aaron or Elizabeth home.

6. Once we get to our destination, I'll call Dad and report progress.

Once you draft your emergency plan, read it aloud to the kids and answer any questions they have. Most likely they'll wonder, "What do I have to do?" Hopefully, the answer will be, "Nothing. We've got it all covered." The idea is to give the adults a specific plan so the lives of the children are disrupted as little as possible. If your children misunderstand a particular step in the plan, consider revising it or adding a step to make it clearer. Knowing they are taken care of and that, no matter what happens, Mom or Dad will be able to handle it is important to kids. They're counting on it.

Leave a space for "Alternatives" on your emergency plan. Maybe a neighbor could pick up Elizabeth from Linda's house when she picks up her own daughter. Then Elizabeth wouldn't have to stay longer than usual. Or maybe Grandma is willing to pick Aaron up at school if Dad is in a meeting. If you list alternatives on your plan, make sure you have the full names and phone numbers of the alternative support people so they can be contacted easily in a fast-moving situation.

Family Emergency Plan

Important Phone Numbers

Police: _____

Fire: _____

Poison control: _____

Mom's work: _____

Dad's work: _____

Friend: _____

Emergency Procedures

1. _____

_____

_____

_____

2. _____
_____
_____
_____

3. _____
_____
_____
_____

4. _____
_____
_____
_____

5. _____
_____
_____
_____

6. _____
_____
_____
_____

Alternatives: _____
_____
_____
_____

Worst:
**"I missed
out on
my son's
firsts."**

The At-Home Emergency Procedure

If your child is home after school by himself, he needs his own set of emergency procedures to follow.

The first step, if you haven't already done so, is to make sure he's clear on what he can and cannot do. Post his after-school rules clearly; they will contribute greatly to his overall safety. Things like, "No cooking on the stove," "Don't answer the front door," and "No swimming," give him guidelines to work with.

Next, devise and discuss a procedure he can follow if he finds himself in an emergency situation. Make sure that he understands what an emergency is and that he knows the most important thing to do in each situation. Here are a few suggestions:

 First aid. Have a first aid kit in a reachable place. Make sure it contains a booklet on simple first-aid procedures (how to treat a burn, what to do for a scrape, etc.).

 Fire. Make sure he knows to get out of the house *first*, and then call 911 (or the number of your local fire department).

Some families write out a fire plan, with a map of the house and surrounding yard, and even practice "fire drills" once in a while to make sure everyone knows what to do in case of fire. You can make this an adventure and have a fire-training course on one of your family meeting nights. Set a loud timer or alarm, then practice leaving the house and meeting up at your designated "safe place" outside.

Storms. Write down what your child should do in the event of a severe storm. Should he go to the basement or to an internal hallway? Where is the safest place in your house? Identify it clearly and explain when it's time to head for cover.

 Strangers. Your child needs to know what to do if a stranger calls or comes to the door. What should he do if he feels threatened? Make sure he has the phone numbers he needs to contact the designated person—the closest neighbor, you, or another friend— who can go check on him if he feels frightened or in danger.

Scary News About Scared Kids

A recent news story related this finding: A lot of American children are scared. Results of a survey showed that they are frightened most of gangs, violence, and guns. In the survey of 7- to 10-year-olds, 71 percent worried they might be stabbed or shot at school.[2]

After-School Rules

Complete these sentences with what you want your child to do in each of these situations:

If you get hurt, _____

_____

If there is a fire, _____

_____

If there is bad weather,_____

_____

If a stranger calls, _____

_____

If a stranger comes to the door, _____
_____

If you are frightened, _____
_____

Once you've completed and posted the after-school rules
(on your information center bulletin board), you can devise
an emergency plan for your at-home child.

At-Home Emergency Plan

Important Phone Numbers

Police: _____

Fire: _____

Poison control: _____

Mom's work: _____

Dad's work: _____

Friend: _____

Emergency Procedures

1. _____
_____
_____
_____

2. _____
_____
_____
_____

3. _____

_____

_____

_____

4. _____

_____

_____

_____

5. _____

_____

_____

_____

6. _____

_____

_____

_____

It's best *not* to include an "Alternatives" section on your child's at-home emergency plan. Options in a time of crisis can be more confusing than helpful. Straightforward, clear instructions— "If this happens, do that"—will be received and followed more easily.

All this talk about emergencies may be unsettling, especially if you're just getting ready to go back to work, or have just started back, and are feeling anxious about the transition. But part of avoiding emergencies is being prepared for them. Your children will feel more secure, and you will feel more at ease knowing that, if something happens, your family has a plan to follow. You will be more relaxed at work knowing you've done everything you can—by way of prevention and education—to avoid those "unforeseen circumstances."

All-Important Permissions

In this day of litigation, giving caregivers permission to get help for your child is an important part of the emergency procedure. If someone else takes care of your child all day, you need to give that person written permission to get medical help for your child in your absence. This doesn't mean you're turning over all your legal rights to someone else. It simply means you give the caregiver the right to authorize emergency medical care as needed until you arrive on the scene. This gives the professionals the legal go-ahead to do whatever is necessary in the case of a dire emergency.

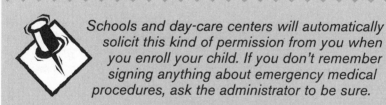

Schools and day-care centers will automatically solicit this kind of permission from you when you enroll your child. If you don't remember signing anything about emergency medical procedures, ask the administrator to be sure.

Write out a simple statement of permission that lists the child's name and age, the caregiver's name, and the date, and sign it at the bottom. It might go something like this:

While _____ is caring for my children (Aaron Amstead, age 7, and Elizabeth Amstead, age 4), I give her permission to authorize emergency medical care in the event that I am unreachable and an accident occurs involving one of my children. I wish to be contacted immediately at _____ in case of such an emergency, but would ask that medical help not be postponed if I am not available.

_____
your signature

You might also list insurance policy numbers, other contact people, or helpful information like allergies or drug sensitivities on the sheet so the attending medical personnel have the information they need about your child.

Summary

In this chapter, you've thought about your expectations and learned about precautions you can take to make your family's transition smoother. You've decided how you want to handle phone calls at work, and mapped out a plan for handling sick days. You've also taken care of basic safety issues and emergency procedures for your family, so everyone is prepared in case an "unforeseen circumstance" appears on your horizon.

Don't let all this "disaster thinking" trouble you. Remember, you're creating these emergency plans to help ensure that emergencies *won't* happen. Once you've got your plan in place, you can sit back and relax. If an emergency ever happens, you'll all know what to do.

Notes

1. Ann Muscari and Wendy Wardell Morrone, *Child Care That Works* (New York: Doubleday, 1989).

2. Matt Lowry, reporting for the "Today Show," December 7, 1995.

Chapter

5

Inside Looking Out

"By working faithfully eight hours a day you may eventually get to be a boss and work twelve hours a day."
—Robert Frost

So you've found the job of your dreams—or, at least, one that will work for now. It meets as many of your family priorities as possible, you've made child-care arrangements, and you're ready to get yourself organized and back to work. There are quite a few accomplishments wrapped up in that one sentence: Take the time to be pleased with your family's accomplishments and cooperation.

This chapter deals with life from a different perspective. Instead of looking out at the work world from the welcoming walls of home, we'll be looking at how to handle home issues from the new environment of the office. But first we'll start with a few basics to help you get into the office with as few bumps and bruises as possible.

Great Expectations

You need to take a good long look at your expectations now that your return to work (or job change) is imminent. If you have unrealistic expectations—"Piece of cake!"—you're going to be disappointed or, worse, feel like you've failed. If you have realistic expectations and know that adjustments take time, that your family is going to need some retraining, and that emotions are going to be in an uproar while everyone gets used to the new system, chances are you'll get through the adjustment period faster and with fewer emotional surprises.

It's easier to steer a ship through a storm when you know the storm is coming and can prepare for it. Anticipating a few storms as you make the big shift from home to work will help you weather them.

Here's a little quiz to test your expectation level.

Back-to-Work Quiz

How difficult do you expect each of the following things to be as you make your adjustment back to work? (1 is easy; 10 is difficult)

___ Finding the right wardrobe for the job

___ Getting home organized so the housework and repairs get done

___ Spending quality time with each child

___ Organizing free time for family events

___ Keeping active in school activities

___ Staying in contact with friends and relatives

___ Finding quiet time for you

When you complete the list, read back through it to make sure you've been as realistic as possible, and don't be surprised if you don't have many 1s. You won't have a whole list of 10s, either—thank goodness! Some things will be comparatively simple, and others will be more difficult. The level of difficulty will vary depending on your circumstances, the type of job you've taken, the ages of your children, and so on. The important thing is this: You should take time to consider what you're expecting of yourself and of your family and ask yourself if your expectations are realistic.

What Do You Feel?

Studies show that returning to the workforce after time at home brings up a number of feelings for both mothers and fathers. Which of these feelings do you have? (Remember that having conflicting feelings is par for the course.)

___ Happy	___ Lonely
___ Sad	___ Eager
___ Excited	___ Irritated
___ Insecure	___ Relieved
___ Contented	___ Anxious
___ Angry	___ Stronger
___ Capable	___ Worried
___ Guilty	___ Proud

Human animals that we are, we also must anticipate the effects of other situations on our emotions. Being overly tired, for example, makes you more prone to feeling sad. You may feel guilty when you've had to say "No" to room mothering but feel fine later in the week when you haven't had to turn down commitments to balance your work responsibilities. You might be short-tempered at home when there's a big deadline at work; or you might have trouble concentrating at your desk when you're worried about your son's first day at the sitter's.

The key to dealing with back-to-work feelings, experts agree, is to feel them. Some days you'll be thankful to get out of the house. Others you might feel sad or lonely. Sometimes, you might wonder if you can handle the pressure. Especially at first, be willing to hang in there with your emotions. Talk to other employees, your employer, your spouse and family, or a professional, if necessary, but let your emotions be what they are. In any time of transition, emotions are high and can shift easily in any direction. Better to wait until things settle down before you start making additional changes.

Remember that you won't be the only one at the office with thoughts other than work on your mind. For you it may be the kids, but for others it might be money, a relationship, graduate work, self-awareness issues, or other things.

How Do You Feel?

It's an interesting medical phenomenon and a proven fact: In times of transition, our immune systems are weakened and we are more likely to pick up colds, the flu, or anything else floating around in the environment. This applies to you and all members of your family. You'll all going through changes together. As you prepare to return to work, keep an eye on each of the following items, which contribute to keeping you all healthy:

1. **Make sure you're getting the rest you need.** Recognize that in times of change—and particularly in times of high stress—you need more rest than usual.

2. **As much as possible, eat well-balanced, healthy meals.** Time for sit-down meals may be shorter than it used to be, and you may wonder if the local fast food drive-through is going to be your standard bill of fare, but try to make sure at least one meal a day is well-balanced, with produce, protein, dairy—you know the scoop. Crock pots and microwaves were invented for people like us. For tips on creating healthy meals on a working-parent schedule, see chapter 8.

3. **Use your supports.** Working parents often suffer from "I-can-do-it-myself" syndrome and find themselves carrying more responsibility

than they really have to. Ask yourself if you
are running errands, washing clothes, drying
dishes, or fielding phone calls someone else
could really take over. Is there someone ready
and willing (or at least enlistable) to take over
some of these tasks during your adjustment
period?

4. **Keep an eye on your caffeine intake.**
Especially when you make a sudden shift from
home to office and are struggling with changes
in schedule, responsibilities, demands, hours,
and expectations, you might notice energy pot-
holes in your day. You were fine a moment ago
and now you're tired. Yawn. You've got all
kinds of things to do this afternoon, and it's not
even 3:00. How can you wake up? A trip to the
coffee machine seems like the answer.

The problem is that too many of those quick
trips—or ones to the alternative, the soft-drink
machine—will pump quite a bit of caffeine into
your system, which will ultimately depress,
not increase, your energy level. People often
think that candy—in particular, chocolate
(that's wishful thinking!)—is a good pick-me-up
for the afternoon sleepies. But chocolate puts
caffeine in your system for a brief time (hence
the pick-me-up feeling) and then causes even
more sleepiness because of the release of
insulin that floods your bloodstream after a
dose of sugar.

More nutrition news than you ever wanted to
know, right? The bottom line is to watch and
moderate whatever you're putting into your
system. Too much of anything—especially
when you're hoping to get a particular reaction
("I've got to wake up!")—can do more harm
than good.

5. **Be alert to your body's signals.** Is your neck
stiff? You might be carrying the "weight of the
world" on your shoulders. Does your head
hurt? You might be focusing too intently for

too long without taking a break. Is your child complaining of stomachaches? Nightmares? Fatigue? Our bodies give us signals when we're working too hard, when we're carrying too much stress, and when we're feeling over-whelmed. Tune into yourself on a regular basis and try to take good care of yourself in the midst of all these changes. When you're hun-gry, eat. When you're tired, sleep. When you've taken work home and you've got 10 pages left to read, but all you really care about is watching the game on TV, watch the game. Being sensitive to your needs is an important key to helping you and your entire family adjust to career changes smoothly.

6. **Take things slow.** One of the hardest expecta-tions we have of ourselves is the one that says we need to have everything handled *now*. Remember that adjusting to work is a process for both you and your family. You'll try a few things in the beginning that just plain won't work. You'll reevaluate and change them. A major task of working parents is assessing what works, weeding out what doesn't, and trying new ideas. It's a rare family that puts a system into place and then maintains it until the kids are grown and the parents retire. Expect your life to be one of continual chang-ing and growing. Every day, you'll make your system a little better. That's a freeing thought: No one says you have to have it all "together" today. You're free to try what works and then change whatever you need to whenever you need to—whether that's this afternoon, next week, or next year.

Expecting the Unexpected

I think the hardest thing for me about returning

to work will be: _____

_____

_____

_____

_____

I could make the situation easier by: _____

_____

_____

_____

_____

I'm Late! I'm Late!

One of the first challenges you'll face on a daily basis is the morning routine. Statistics show that working parents have a higher percentage of tardiness than nonparenting workers—both late *to* work and late *leaving* work.[1] In fact, it's estimated that between 40 and 70 percent of working parents wind up adjusting their schedules—at least temporarily—because of home delays and unanticipated crises. ("Where's my lunch box? It was here a minute ago!" "*Mom!* I can't find my other shoe!")

One of the best things about being disorganized is that it teaches you the value of organization. After the third time Scott can't find his homework and it makes you late for a meeting, you're going to insist that he gather his schoolwork in his bookbag and put it by the door every night before he goes to bed.

Learning from our mistakes is valuable—but learning from other's mistakes saves us a lot of frustration. Consider what these parents say about getting out the door in the morning:

❖ ❖

"Getting out on time is the hardest thing I face all day. I figure that once I get all three kids up, dressed, fed, and delivered to school and the baby-sitter, I've already succeeded for the day. I go to work feeling great."
—Mother of three who works full-time

❖ ❖

"Get school clothes, backpacks, books, and everything you need for the next day ready the night before. This really helps get us out in the morning."
—Mother of three who works part-time

❖ ❖

"Get organized! Have things ready the night before. No matter how organized you are, things can pop up and destroy what you've accomplished. My husband travels occasionally and things always break when he's gone: the windows leak on a rainy day, the dog gets hit by a car, our daughter throws up when I'm ready to walk out the door to work. When things get overwhelming, I take a deep breath and say, "Okay, Lord, I can only handle a little more of this!"
—Mother of two who works full-time

In chapter 7, you will learn some ways you can organize your house to spread out household chores and earn yourself a little sanity. Here, the "organization" I'm talking about is really time management. How can you get yourself organized in the morning so you can get out the door on time?

Working Backwards

The first step is to determine how much time you need in order to walk in the door at work every day with a few minutes to spare. Think about how nice that would be—no more rushing through the door, sneaking past the boss's office, or hoping the receptionist didn't notice you're late yet another day this week.

If you make a commitment to yourself to be on time, you're more likely to be on time. If you don't think being punctual on your job is particularly important, chances are you'll continue to scurry in 10 minutes late this day, 20 minutes the next. The choice, of course, is yours. But remember that bosses consider this kind of thing when you ask for additional time off, schedule vacation days, or put in for a promotion.

So, to determine how much time you need to get to work on time, answer these questions:

1. **What time do you need to be at work?** If starting time is 8:00 A.M., plan to be in 10 minutes early. This gives you time to get your coffee, look through your mail, and settle into the day without feeling rushed.

2. **How long is your commute?** If the length of your commute varies depending on the day—for example, you drop Taylor off at day care on Tuesdays and Thursdays, which adds 10 minutes to your trip—figure this out for each day that differs.

3. **How many children do you have?** (If you have to stop and count, you're in trouble!) Whatever number you come up with, leave 5 minutes *per child* for getting-to-the-car-in-one-piece time. If you have three children, leave a 15-minute space to absorb Katie forgetting to brush her teeth, Ian needing to change the brown sock he thought was blue, and Sara running back for her show-and-tell offering.

4. **How long does it take your family to eat breakfast?** Some people eat on the run, others eat in the car. Some don't eat at all. Whatever your breakfast practice is, schedule it and know how long it takes.

5. **How much time does your family need to get ready in the morning?** This might be a hard one to measure and will probably require some observation and perhaps some reorchestration. If your house has two teenagers, two adults, and one bathroom, and you all need to get showers in the morning (not to mention mirror time for things like hair curling and make-up routines), it's going to be hard on your schedule—not to mention your nerves. You may need to think about alternative ways to make sure everybody gets ready on time. Younger children usually don't mind

taking baths or showers at night—in fact, mine prefer it if they think it will delay bedtime— but older kids might feel put off their routine.

 If you suspect there's a better way to orchestrate your "getting ready" time, put the issue on the table at the next family meeting and see what alternatives your family can come up with. You might be surprised at the creative answers you receive.

Once you figure out the time you need for each part of your morning routine, add them up and see what the total tells you. Then subtract the total from the time you need to be at work and you've got the time you need to set your alarm for. The following checklist gives you an example of the basic equation. A blank checklist is provided at the end of this section for you to fill in your own times.

Time I need to be at work: 7:50

Commute:	20 minutes
Time cushion:	15 minutes
Breakfast:	15 minutes
Getting ready:	45 minutes
TOTAL TIME:	**1 hour, 35 minutes**

Time I need to get up: 6:15

Time Management Checklist

Time I need to be at work: _____

Commute: _____

Time cushion: _____

Breakfast: _____

Getting ready: _____

TOTAL TIME: _____

Time I need to get up: _____

One quick warning: *If you come up with an answer like, "We need three hours to get ready for work and school, and we have to be there by 7:45. That means I need to get up at 4:45!"—then you need to do some reorganizing to reduce the amount of time you need in the morning. The next section will tell you how.*

BEST & WORST

Best: "The kids are more independent— never upset about going to school, etc."

Early Morning Organization

Don't let the heading fool you. What we're talking about here really isn't organization you do in the morning. Rather, it's things you do the night before (or all week) that help you be better organized in the morning.

Most families, no matter how long they've been doing the to-work-and-to-school routine, still have days when they oversleep, the dog doesn't get fed, the kids forget their homework, and everyone gets stuck in traffic. It's going to happen.

But there are a number of things you can do to get yourself and your family ready for tomorrow morning with fewer hassles and headaches. Consider these:

 Do everything you can the night before. Don't put off until tomorrow what you can do tonight—not if you want to have a smooth exit in the morning. Sign school papers or assignment books, check homework, read through reports, pack swimming gear, make lunches. Whatever it is that eats up your time in the morning, see if you can handle it the night before.

 Have a going-out place. Typically families use one exit regularly—whether it's the door leading to the garage or one leading to the school bus. Wherever your family exits, make sure they've got their belongings there waiting for them. You might even add coat hooks, mitten places, a mat for boots and tennis shoes, and room for other niceties like umbrellas or mufflers, so you can grab everything you need on your way out the door.

 If you want to save time and energy, teach your kids (and your spouse, if necessary) to be responsible for packing their own things for tomorrow. They can put the bookbags (or briefcases) by the door, get the library books, the swim bags, the show-and-tell items, and have them ready to head out the door.

 Designate an information center. Hang a bulletin board or reserve counter space by the door for notes that need to be signed, papers that need to be returned, or items that need parental approval. Use this area also for important items you might need to find at a moment's notice: things like your number at work, emergency phone numbers, and your family's activity calendar.

 Be day-ahead clothes conscious. Make sure the next day's clothes (and shoes, socks, and underwear) are set out, ready to be slipped on at a moment's notice.

 Use a color-coded calendar to list family activities. You might want to hang this calendar in your "information center." Use a different color marker for each person in the family. When Sean has swimming on Wednesdays, you'll see the blue ink (when you check Tuesday night) and know you've got to put his swimsuit and towel in a bag by the going-out door. The most important thing about the family calendar, of course, is that you use it regularly, and teach all other family members to do the same. When Steven needs a ride home after the game on Friday, make sure he writes it in (and asks you, too), so he will be picked up when and where he expects to be.

Our Ready List

Things we can have ready each night before bed:

1. _____

2. _____

3. _____

4. _____

5. _____

6. _____

7. _____

8. _____

9. _____

10. _____

The Commute

Ah, you made it. The kids are safely at school or the baby-sitter's, and you are on your way to work. Looks like you'll have plenty of time. Traffic is moving smoothly and there's nothing ominous on the horizon. Now is a good time to leave the morning behind and get ready—mentally—to start your workday.

Depending on the length of your commute and your circumstances—whether you drive alone, carpool, or use public transportation—you can use your commute time to organize your day and priorities, think about creative projects you're looking forward to, or ponder challenges you need creative answers for.

Some people use these few moments of precious quiet as "preparation time" for the day. You might listen to music or inspirational tapes, meditate or pray, or just notice the beauty of the changing sunrise. If you feel you need a few minutes of silence before (or in the midst of) a busy day, don't rob yourself of the opportunity. A few deep breaths, a few moments of quiet thought (or, even better, no thought), and you may be surprised how refreshed and ready you'll feel.

If you have trouble leaving home at home and find yourself worrying about your new baby-sitter, wondering whether you handed John's lunch to Tammy and Tammy's to John, or fretting that you forgot to close the door to the hamster's cage, you might want to try carrying a small notebook—or getting one of those that attach directly to your dashboard—and writing down the item you need to follow up on at home. When you write it down, see yourself mentally putting it out of your mind. There. It's on the paper. Now you don't have to let it crowd your thoughts. You can add it to your "to-do" list once you get to the office, and when you call home to check in later, you can follow up on the things you're concerned about. For now, let it go.

If you find that something keeps bothering you day after day and that writing it down and checking on it later doesn't seem to dispel the worry, take it as a sign that you need to do some further investigating. Maybe something in your system isn't working. If you are worrying about Jessica every morning after you drop her off at day care, take a closer look at what worries you. Is it the look on her face when you leave? Is it the way she interacts with her teachers? Listen to your instincts and follow up on your feelings. Perhaps she needs a few more minutes with you—a slower transition from home to school. Maybe there are some questions you can ask her caregivers that will alleviate your worries. Don't just shrug off concerns that rise to the surface again and again. Chances are, there's something you can learn that will make the situation better for all of you.

Did I Tell You About the Time . . . ?

"When my children were infants, I always felt so strongly about their morning feeding. That closeness was so important to me to start the day. So I'd be dressed and ready for work before that feeding. Many times I'd get to work and someone would tell me that I had something running down my back—it was spit up. I'd walk around all day branded, smelling like sour milk!"

—Mother of two who works full-time

Really at Work

Knowing that your children are safely provided for—and that procedures are in place to take care of even the most stressful situations—earns you peace of mind at work. You can concentrate on what's before you, which makes you more productive and ensures your success on the job.

The ability to be "really at work" comes quickly to some, more slowly to others. It has something to do with how ready you were to return to work. If you have changed jobs or returned to the workforce because you had to, tearing yourself away from home mentally and emotionally probably is harder. You might resist the idea of leaving home behind. If you were eager to get back into the workforce and felt ready for it, your power of concentration is apt to be stronger sooner.

In any case, be gentle with yourself as you adjust to the working world. These tips might help compartmentalize thoughts of home during your transition time so you can be productive and still feel connected to your family:

End each work hour with a 5-minute "family-thought break." If you're supposed to be writing a report, and instead find your mind wandering to the cookies you plan to bake with Emily on Saturday morning, remind yourself that it's not "family-thought" time and even make a note, if necessary, to think about the ingredients you need for the cookies at the designated break. No employer will begrudge you 5 minutes of daydreaming an hour if it makes you more productive the other 55 minutes.

 Surround yourself with drawings and pictures the kids have made for your office. Bring in clay sculptures, photographs, or whatever makes you feel more "at home" in your work area.

Did I Tell You About the Time . . . ?

For part of one summer, I took over the management of a retail museum shop. After eight years as a work-at-home mom, I was having a hard time with the adjustment. My then-6-year-old son Christopher had the answer. One morning, while I was making a sad exit to work, he came rushing up with something behind his back. "Here Mom," he said, thrusting a well-loved Ernie doll into my free hand, "Ernie can go to work with you so you won't miss me so much." Ernie did go to work with me, and sat on my desk the rest of the summer. The artists and sales reps who met with me probably thought my taste in "art" was a little weird, but my heart felt better.

 Seek out other working parents. When you are introduced to fellow employees, be alert to pictures of children, comments about kids or pets, or other signs that they might be working parents. At break time or lunch time, start a conversation. Chances are, they've felt just what you're feeling about starting a new job and balancing home and work. They might be able to give a few pointers that will help make the transition a smoother one, or at least give you an idea of how your employer responds to family adjustments.

 Be proud of your family and your accomplishments. Although the emotional tide is turning, not too long ago we easily adopted an apologetic attitude when discussing our families. The prevalent feeling was that being first-rate parents made us second-rate employees. Today, more and more companies are recognizing the value of hiring employees with a strong sense of family commitment. That commitment can translate to more responsibility, loyalty, and creativity on the job.

 When you are at work, work. Especially when you first make other working-parent friends at work, the temptation might be strong to share the latest cute story, the newest teacher complaint, or the most outrageous Christmas wish. Remember, above all else, that the balance of home and work means you need to be home when you're home and at work when you're at work—physically, emotionally, and mentally. Employers will see even more benefit in hiring employees with family priorities if they are pleased with the return they get on their investment. In short, share kid stories on your own time and when you're at work, work.

Coming Home

In your first few weeks back to work, leaving work at work might not be difficult at all. You may be itching to get out the door and make sure everything is okay with the kids. After a few weeks, you'll fall into a routine. Your basic fears

**BEST &
WORST**

Worst:
"Not being
there when
my son
gets off the
schoolbus."

will have been allayed, you'll see what works and what doesn't, and you'll have made some changes to correct the things that haven't been working the way you expected.

With your system basically in place, your mind will be free to get more invested in your job. Now is when you discover if you're an "after-work worrier" or a "forget-about-it-till-morning" personality type.

You can use the commute home to make the transition between the work world and the happy chaos of incomplete homework, marshmallow squares, and mismatched socks.

How do you let the day go? Deep breathing works. Even in the worst traffic, you can feel the stress subsiding with a few deep breaths. Make a checklist of things you need to follow up on at the office in the morning, if the office keeps intruding on your thoughts. As you write down the notes, consider them "taken care of" and give yourself permission to enjoy your evening with your family. You'll have plenty of time to address work issues again tomorrow, beginning bright and early at 8:00 A.M.

Summary

You've taken a big step—perhaps the biggest step in establishing a home-and-work balance. You've made the transition from home to work by recognizing what a terrific adjustment you're going through and making sure you have the time and resources in place to deal with your changing days.

The next chapter tells you what you can expect once the honeymoon period ends. You can count on some turbulence, but nothing you can't navigate with a little foresight, love, and tenacity.

Notes

1. Ann Muscari and Wendy Wardell Morrone,
    Child Care That Works (New York: Doubleday,
    1989).

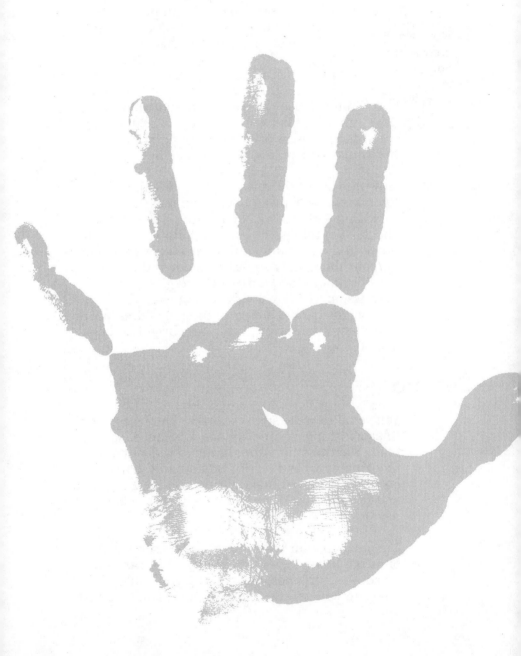

Chapter

6

Post-Parting Blues

"There's no such thing as fun for the entire family."
—Jerry Seinfeld

You may be feeling a little skeptical right now. Sure, family priorities, you're thinking. Yeah, that mission statement *really* helped. How come Kim has started wetting the bed again and Max has been getting in trouble at school? Why isn't the house getting any cleaner? Will there ever be a day when I get to work on time? Will there ever be a morning when I don't have to stand in a cold shower just to get my eyes open? I'm not sure my boss likes me.

I'm not sure my kids like me. I don't think the dog likes me. Come to think of it, even *I'm* not too crazy about me.

The Honeymoon's Over

Let's recap what has happened here. You got your priorities in line and set out to find the job that matched them.

Good.

You found just the right child care and organized with your spouse on getting the kids to and from the caregiver's house, day care, or school.

Terrific. We're really getting somewhere.

Next, you made the big move into the office. You covered all the bases for keeping the lines of communication open and making sure everyone knew the plan for handling emergency situations. You figured out how to leave home at home and, at the end of the day, work at work.

There you were, finally, a working parent. Life was all organized and everyone knew what he or she was supposed to do. A magnificent accomplishment!

For two or three blissful days—or perhaps a week or more, if you were lucky—there was a happy little thought bouncing around in your head: "We can do this! This is working!"

Then it all began to unravel.

What Have I Done?

The unraveling probably started slowly. The dog got sick. Kim threw her first temper tantrum as you dropped her off for day care. Max missed the bus to school.

A deadline at work came and went. You didn't get the report finished on time. Your spouse had to work overtime and you had to leave early to get Kim from child care. Max overflowed the toilet and couldn't find the plunger.

Continue adding up these minor incidents and pretty soon you've got what feels like total meltdown. Combine that with your own fatigue, disappointment, and worry, and you've set yourself up for a bad case of What Have I *DONE*?!

It's Normal

We humans are complex creatures: When we go through periods of change, we are adjusting on several different levels. When you do something as drastic as change jobs or return to work (which ranks right up there with having a baby, losing a loved one, or going through a divorce as a stress-inducer), you are adjusting emotionally, physically, and mentally. All these are interrelated; which means the more you worry, the more tired you are. The more you add to your daily schedule, the more worn down you become. The more you use your brain, the more you need time to rest it.

Being run down—temporarily or continually—has a dramatic effect on you as a complete package: your emotions are more volatile and less consistent; your physical stamina is noticeably lessened; and your mental sharpness blurs into a fog that may really alarm you at work.

The answer? Realize how much you've changed and commit to taking good care of yourself while you adjust. Rest more, eat right. Sleep whenever you can—at least seven and a half hours a night.

When you take better care of you, you'll have more emotional wherewithal to deal with your rebelling children and your angry dog. If you don't take care of yourself, the emotions of everyone else will flatten you like a steamroller on hot asphalt.

 Chapter 8 is all about finding time for yourself—in both big and small ways—in the midst of a hectic, harried lifestyle. It's possible. I promise.

It's easy to neglect our own needs without even knowing we're doing it. But it's where you need to start rethreading when life begins to unravel. Take this quick quiz to see if you've been caring for yourself:

Self-Care Quiz

How many times this week did you...

___ tell yourself you did a good job?

___ do something you really wanted to do?

___ feel proud of an accomplishment?

___ eat a well-balanced meal?

___ rest in the afternoon?

___ go to bed early just because you felt like it?

___ accept a well-deserved compliment?

___ let someone help you when they offered?

___ do something just for fun?

It's Temporary

This slump you've fallen into is part of the overall adjustment period. It may look like the kids weren't being sincere when they said they'd help with household chores, take messages, get along, and generally cooperate with the changes taking place. But remember, they are going through a pushing-and-testing-and-generally-out-of-sorts phase, too.

You've heard the phrase, "This too shall pass"? It applies here, too.

Know What to Expect

In the last chapter, we talked about expectations: what you expected of yourself and of your family as you made your first steps back into the workforce. What we didn't address there—because it fits here—is the issue of adjustment expectations.

Some of us live life with a "been-there, done-that" philosophy. We think that once we've accomplished something, we should be able to pack it away in our bag of "learned" things. We shouldn't have to learn it all over again.

If we apply this philosophy to ourselves as parents—and, in particular, as working parents— we're never going to measure up to our own expectations. We're not going to accept that learning to be a working parent—to balance home and work successfully—is an ongoing process that takes continual fine-tuning and reassessment. We're going to think, "We should have mastered this by now," and beat ourselves up (or get really upset with our families) when the situation spirals out of our control.

The solution is simple. Especially in this adjustment period, be grateful for the way your family is pulling together, even if they seem to be pulling together in separate directions. Find small things to be thankful for, even if you need a microscope. Notice how the kids are trying and make a lot of noise about that. And correct the rebellions or misunderstandings directly but without a lot of fanfare.

When you see this difficult time as part of the overall adjustment cycle, it becomes easier to weather. As one mother put it,

"Try not to over-focus on failures that are insignificant. Choose your battles wisely—if you choose to engage in a power struggle with your child, make sure it's worth the bloodshed."
—Mother of two who works full-time

BEST & WORST

Best:
"Being away from my children during the day makes me cherish the time that we do have together so much more. It makes me so thankful that I have a wonderful family to go home to."

Whatever Can Go Wrong, Will

This is an old recast of Murphy's Law, expressing not so much an expectation as a perspective on how we can look at the "wrong" things that happen in our lives.

I'm not suggesting you should expect things to go wrong, but we do have a choice of how we react when they do. If we understand that our system is going to be tested—that things will break down, the kids will fight, this one will miss the car pool, that one will break the rules—maybe we won't overreact when things go wrong. We will see the breakdowns not as something we've failed to orchestrate or control but, rather, as part of the natural process of adjustment that is happening in our families.

Not that enforceable offenses—broken household rules, blatant violations, refused chores—shouldn't be dealt with; they should. But having the proper perspective on the "wrongs" when they happen helps you address the problem clearly.

Looking at Wrong the Right Way

If you look at your back-to-work adjustment as a continual process, you'll see that your system breaks down only where it needs reinforcement. The "wrongs" then become the weak links that need to be addressed. Each time you find something that doesn't work, you can see it as another way to make your system stronger.

If Patrick isn't calling you after school at the prescribed time, you need to assess why. Consider where the rule is breaking down. Is he simply disregarding your rules? Is it a difficult time for him to get to the phone? Is there another reason you don't know about? Talking with Patrick will help you assess the situation and make any necessary changes or additions.

Challenges at Home

The first place you're likely to be tested is on the home front. Things aren't the way they used to be, and change always causes some resistance. You can save yourself from fighting the resistance effort by thinking about your family rules and deciding which ones you need to keep, which ones need to go, and which ones should be revised.

Family Rules

What are your family rules? Each family is different, but most of us have some rules in common. We have determined what time the kids need to be in bed, whether Joe can watch TV before his homework is done, how long Erica can talk on the phone after dinner, and what kind of snacking we allow between meals. We have set curfews, decided on room cleaning issues, and drawn the lines of responsibility around family chores and allowances.

But do you have the rules in writing? If you already have your family rules written down and posted on the refrigerator, good for you—you're a few steps ahead of the rest of us. Many parents have learned that rules that are simply stated— "Christa, I told you to be in bed by 9:00!"—can be easily bent: "But, Mom, I thought you meant in bed *reading* by 9:00!"

If you have written rules—well-thought-out, clearly written rules—the verbal loopholes won't be open. Your kids won't be able to say, "But Mom, I thought . . . " and knock you off your resolve. Write them down and put them up. It will make the up-front aspect of your communications much clearer. Your kids—and you—will be able to see in black and white what you meant.

If you looked into the home lives of 100 working parents, you'd see a wide range of parenting styles: strict and permissive, liberal and conservative. You'd find people who spank and people who don't. You'd find parents who yell and children who yell back. You'd discover families in which kids are in control, families in which parents are in control, and families in which nobody (except perhaps the dog) is in control. Such is the nature of modern life. It's not a judgment, it's just fact: Whatever works for you, works for you. The main thing is to keep trying. Sooner or later you'll run across the tools, knowledge, insight, and/or experience you need to put together the system that works for you.

Our Family Rules

1. _____
2. _____
3. _____
4. _____
5. _____
6. _____
7. _____
8. _____
9. _____
10. _____

A few tips for creating your rule sheet:

 If you name one child in a rule, name them all (or rewrite the rule to omit names entirely). If Rule #3 is "Erica must wash the dinner dishes before she can talk on the phone," change it to "Phone time is allowed only after the dishes have been done," to avoid singling out one child. Or if this is a rule that applies only to Erica, make sure you've got one that applies only to her brother, as well: "Joe must finish his homework before watching TV."

 Use positive wording. Nobody wants to read a list of don'ts. "Don't raid the refrigerator while Dad and I are at work" becomes "Eat only the snacks I've set out on the counter for you."

 Think about the most important issues and write them into your rules. Which issues cause you the most consternation? These are the ones you need to be clearest about. A well-written rule can end all the "But, Mom . . . " hassle you've been wrestling with.

 Know that your rules will be tested and broken. As you write the rules, be realistic and reasonable. Remember that the primary purpose of making rules is to create guidelines your children will ultimately enforce themselves—not to overload them with standards they can't live up to.

 Be ready with consequences for broken rules. The consequence should be logically linked to the crime, and they should be written on the rule sheet so the kids know what they're setting themselves up for before they break the rules.

 Expect resistance. If you've never done anything like this before, expect grumbling. If you've got teenagers, you might hear something like, "I suppose you want to control how many times a minute I *breathe* now." With smaller kids, you may get varied reactions, from "Aw, Mom" to a willing attitude, a feeling that this might be "fun," or even some sense of relief.

 Information is power, and when your kids know—and see in black and white—what you expect of them, they will be relieved on some level. They won't have to guess where the boundaries are. At first they may think this limits their freedom, but your clarity about family rules will make life easier for everyone.

Rules and Consequences

There's a problem. "We could handle it this way," your spouse says, as you discuss your son's impending punishment. "We could just ground him for a month and that would be the end of it!" you exclaim.

In most cases, rules are actually solutions. A problem pops up and you create a rule to keep it from popping up again. If you've been waiting for an important call and the caller finally contacts you at work and says, "I've tried the last three nights to get through on your home line, but it's always busy," you know you have a problem with phone use.

A rule can solve this. "Your phone time is now 7:00 P.M. to 8:00 P.M., Sandra," you say to the 14-year-old with the phone growing out of her ear. You revise the rule sheet to include the new rule. But simply setting the rule doesn't necessarily mean the battle's over. Rules were made to be—and will be—tested.

Experts tell us that effective rule setting—coupled with the foresight that things will undoubtedly crop up to challenge the rules—makes a tremendous difference in how quickly your family begins pulling together.[1] When you set the rules for your family, follow this three-pronged approach:

Every rule should address a particular problem.

Every rule should have logical consequences.

Every rule should be reviewed on a regular basis.

What's the Problem?

Now that you're back at work, you may need to think about either modifying your existing rules or officially writing them down for the first time.

Start with a list of problems you need to address:

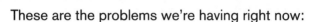

Rules Worksheet, Part I

These are the problems we're having right now:

1. _____

2. _____

3. _____

4. _____

5. _____

Your list might involve problems like these:

1.   Derrick has invited friends to the house twice after he's been told no one is allowed in while we're gone.

2.   Casey refuses to take naps at the baby-sitter's.

3.   Megan is not doing her chores.

4.   Ben has missed the bus three times in the last two weeks, making me late for work.

5.   Luke has been in trouble for fighting at preschool.

What's the Answer?

Look at each entry on your list and consider how it could be reworded into a rule. For example, the first issue could be made into a rule that reads,

1. Friends are allowed in the house only when Mom or I are home.

Go through your list, turning the problem statements into solution statements (your new rules).

Rules Worksheet, Part II

These rules address the problems we've been having:

1. _____
2. _____
3. _____
4. _____
5. _____

What's the Consequence?

Now that you've identified what's going wrong in your system (or, more positively, where your opportunities for improvement lie), and turned the problems into rules, you need to think about the consequences that will result when the rules are broken.

The best consequences—the ones that teach cause and effect—are linked to the broken rule in some logical way. When Casey refuses to take a nap at the baby-sitter's, the logical consequence might be an earlier bedtime or a rest time when she gets home at the end of the day.

There are as many potential consequences as there are circumstances. You may need to give quite a bit of thought to the best reaction for the action. In the case of Casey and the refused naps, for example, there could be other things at play. Maybe she doesn't really need the nap. Perhaps the room she's resting in is too noisy. Maybe a quiet time during which she looks at a picture book or listens to music would be enough. Try to look at the entire picture when you define the problem. And know why you've chosen a consequence before you set it up as part of your system.

Rules Worksheet, Part III

If you break this rule: _____

Expect this: _____

If you break this rule: _____

Expect this: _____

If you break this rule: _____

Expect this: _____

If you break this rule: _____

Expect this: _____

If you break this rule: _____

Expect this: _____

The age of your child will determine the rules and consequences he is able to understand and follow. While removing privileges works well for older children, preschoolers are just learning the principle of cause and effect. For the younger set, you might set up consequences like time-out, which stops the negative behavior, sets clear boundaries, and lets the child start again.[2]

When Should You Revise the Rules?

The process of setting family rules is continual. As your children grow, and as your family settles into a routine and gets through the acclimation period, your rules will change as old problems are solved and new ones arise.

You'll soon discover that you have two different kinds of rules: *foundational rules* and *situational rules*. Foundational rules are the basic, no-kidding rules that your family lives by no matter what. These will not change, and you want to be sure your children know they are important to you.

Situational rules you develop in answer to specific problems. Problems like Casey refusing to nap or Sandra's marathon phone conversations are solved with situational rules. When the problem goes away, the rule can go, too. Of course, if the problem returns, the rule can be put back into effect.

The key to knowing when to revise situational rules—to remove one, add another, or edit one you've already got—is simply to be observant. When Casey starts napping again, for example, you'll know the problem is solved, at least for now, and can be removed from the rule list. Removing situational rules is a good thing. Don't just keep adding to the list until it covers the front of your refrigerator. Better to remove the rules as they are no longer needed. Everyone will understand that the rules are there for a reason—they help the family answer a problem—and that when the problem is solved, the rule is no longer needed. The kids will see rules as solutions to situations, not as an arbitrary form of parental control.

A Final Word

It may seem impossible, but the best way to weather this trying period at home is to (1) expect challenges, (2) prepare solutions, (3) remember that this too shall pass, and (4) keep your sense of humor.

Focusing on the positive things your children are doing to help your back-to-work transition—even if you need to go on a treasure hunt to find them—will encourage the kids to do more. Let the rules take care of the things they *aren't* doing; no more nagging, no more exasperation. If they break the rule, they pay the consequence. This leaves you free to focus on the things they *are* doing well: how well they're doing at school, how straight they're keeping their rooms, how promptly they got off the phone after their phone time, how pleasant they were at dinner.

Being a positive parent is a lot more fun than being a negative parent. Designing and implementing a good set of family rules lets you remove yourself from law enforcement and concentrate on the nurturing, teaching, and loving parts of the job.

Challenges at Work

Having things go haywire at home is bad enough, but things aren't working well on the job, either. You missed your first big deadline. Your boss is looking at you like she thinks she may have made a mistake. The guy in the next cubicle made a comment yesterday about how "sweet" it is that your daughter calls you at work every 15 minutes. Somehow you suspect he doesn't really think it's sweet.

Although the family rule system you're implementing may be new, at least you have a past history to work with. Whether your rules were written and posted on the fridge (or bulletin board) or not, your family had already been working with an established—if only verbal—set of rules.

Work is a different story. You've just gotten this job, so you're not sure what to expect. There are many variables—people, projects, learning curves—and you've somehow got to navigate all of them and still get your work done.

BEST &
WORST

Worst:
"The fatigue factor: not much is left at the end of the day."

Great Expectations

First and foremost, accept that you are going through some major adjustments. Allow yourself to feel a little off your game: Don't expect perfection. Chances are, you expect much more of yourself than anyone around you is expecting right now.

What's the Problem?

Next, assess the problem. Where is your new work system breaking down? What are your issues? Get them down on paper where you can see them clearly.

Work Issues

These are the things I'm having trouble with at work:

1. _____

2. _____

3. _____

4. _____

5. _____

Your list might include problems like this:

1.　I can't figure out the e-mail system.

2.　I don't have time to get all my work done.

3.　The deadlines are stressing me out.

4.　I feel isolated and alone.

5.　I don't know if I'm up to this.

6.　My office mate is hard to get along with.

Whatever the issue, know that there is something you can do about it. Sometimes just making the list—getting the problems identified—can help you figure out the answer.

Resolving Work Issues

Now that you've got your list, look carefully at each problem statement, one at a time. Does a solution automatically come to mind? Do you think, "I could try this," or, "Maybe she could help"?

Often when we allow ourselves to brainstorm answers to a situation, many different answers come. Using your "problem statement" list, write a new list, leaving blank space between each entry. Then give yourself 15 or 20 minutes of quiet time (a lunch break, a coffee break, or any other period during which you won't be interrupted) and read through each issue on your list. Read the statement and ask yourself, "What can I do about this?" Then write down any and all answers that come to you. You can weed them out and choose the ones you want to try later.

Resolving Work Issues

Problem: _____

Possible solutions: _____

Problem: _____

Possible solutions: _____

Problem: _____

Possible solutions: _____

From One Parent to Another
"Experience is a great teacher, and your kids will grow up understanding more about your occupation than they will about any other types of jobs. But if you take your children to the office, be sure to do it in age-appropriate chunks. Take your 2-year-old in for a quick appearance while you pick up that file you forgot, for example, or let your 6-year-old sort your colored paper clips while you run off a few copies. But don't take the kids in for hours at a time and expect them to be happy and entertained. It's not their world, and the amusement won't last long."
—Mother of three who works full-time

Once you have a list of possible solutions, you can decide on a plan of action. This involves weeding out the solutions you think are less likely to work, the ones you don't want to try first, or the ones that are totally impractical (like winning the lottery and quitting your job).

What makes a good solution? Only you know the answer to that question. It will depend on what's most important to you, the circumstances surrounding your challenge, and what you're trying to accomplish. The most important thing is to define your problem, know that there is a resolution in there somewhere, and to give yourself the time and space to think creatively and let the answer reveal itself. You can then implement whichever solutions seem to fit the circumstance, whether you need to ask for help, reorganize your work time, communicate more directly with your coworkers or employer, or find friends for support and encouragement.

Balance Is a Verb

If you're like many working parents, there are days you feel like you're walking a tightrope with a baby on your hip and a briefcase in your hand. Beneath you, a hundred feet down, stand all the other people who depend on you: your spouse, your boss, your family, your friends, your clients. You feel all eyes on you. The pressure is tremendous.

The balancing act will continue because many things are important to us and we are continually called to align ourselves with our values and our priorities. Take heart in the knowledge that we're all walking the same rope. The balancing doesn't stop, but it does get easier.

And while we're up here, we might as well have a little fun with it. Finesse is in order. Daring spins and turns will amuse the audience and make your act uniquely yours. In all the pressures and pitfalls of being a working parent, there is something authentically yours about the system you create. Be yourself, have fun with it, and create a system that reflects the best you and your family can do.

Summary

Soon after you begin your job, no matter how perfect everything seems, life begins to unravel. Not only do things start going wrong at home, but the office may seem threatening, as well. But, as this chapter has outlined, there are a number of ways you can assess what's happening and set about making your family system stronger. And you can apply the same problem-solving techniques to figure out your challenges at work and devise a plan to meet them.

The next chapter concentrates on organizing your home so things get done more smoothly with less effort from you. Do less and get more done. Doesn't that sound nice?

Notes

1. Kenneth Kaye, *Family Rules* (New York: St. Martin's Press, 1984), pp. 33-83.

2. The clearest, most helpful book I've found on setting time-out limits is *Time-Out for Toddlers* by Dr. James W. Varni and Donna G. Corwin (New York: Berkley Books, 1991).

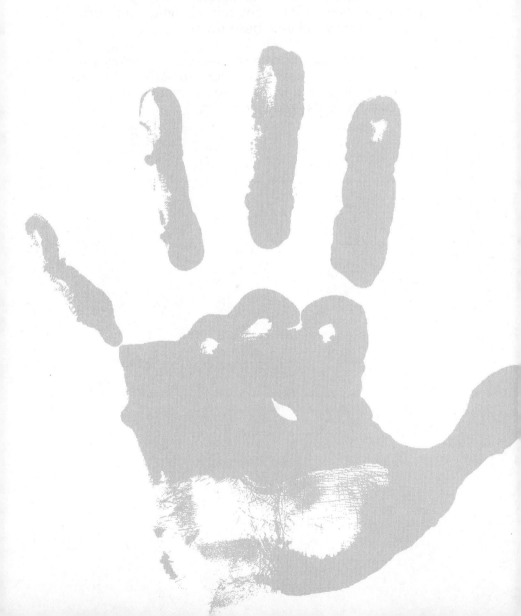

On the Home Front

"I hate housework! You make the beds, you do the dishes—and six months later you have to start all over again."
—Joan Rivers

Things are on the upswing. Home life is settling down. Life at the office seems more manageable and less overwhelming. The kids are beginning to understand the importance of their willing participation during this adjustment period, and you and your spouse are generally happy with the family priorities you've set. You are working well together to get everybody where they need to be at the times they need to be there.

Then one day you pull into the driveway and notice a shutter hanging by a single bolt. "I've got to fix that," you say to yourself, making a mental note. A week later, your daughter says, "Did you notice that one of the shutters is falling off the house?" Oops. You forgot. Another week passes, and the shutter is in the bushes. You stand out front and consider your options. "Doesn't look that bad," you think. "Maybe I should just take all the shutters down. Then I don't have to mess with them."

Getting things done around the house is difficult even when life isn't turned up to a frantic pace. Now, more than ever, you need to organize. You need a system to be sure that everything that needs to be done is done and—more importantly— that you don't do it all yourself.

From One Parent to Another

"Get your children to help. If each child does just one thing (puts clothes away, washes the dishes, empties the dishwasher), it makes things so much easier."
—Mother of four who works part-time

The House Is Calling—Loudly

You may have become aware your house needs TLC in a not-so-gentle fashion. Perhaps your son called you at work one day. "Three different lawn care companies called this morning, Mom," he said. "Do you think someone's trying to tell us it's time to cut the grass?"

Or maybe the pastor knocked at the door and you found yourself rushing around the family room, trying frantically to brush the cat hair off the sofa and pick the cracker crumbs off the rug.

Or perhaps your in-laws stopped by unexpectedly, and you began devising ways to keep them out of the kitchen, where dishes were still stacked from dinner the night before.

Life is messy, with or without kids. Everyone has a junk drawer, a monster closet that threatens to spill out into the hallway, or a corner (or room) that just seems to collect broken things. Some of us are more disorganized than others, and some of us don't have a clue how to start digging out.

This chapter helps you come up with practical responses to the practical issues that are bound to crop up as a result of the new demands on your ever-more-precious time. One way to answer household challenges is to enlist help. Another answer is to organize, organize, organize—put a system in place so your house is straight-with-occasional-clutter instead of cluttered-with-occasional-straight-places.

Fire prevention vs. fire-fighting

It's not usually the way the world works, but it's a lot easier to implement a solution to a problem *before* you have the problem. You might even be able to avoid the problem altogether.

Case in point: organizing at home. If you begin organizing after everything explodes and you can't find something you really need, you're organizing in fire fighting mode. ("Things are really a mess! I've got to do something about this!") But if you look around one afternoon and say, "Hmmm. I'll bet there's an easier way to do this," you can begin calmly to organize your life and your house a little at a time. This second approach—fire prevention as opposed to fire fighting—is much gentler and easier to follow through with in the long run.

Basic Housework 101

Chances are, you've been doing housework for years. Soon after your return to work, you'll notice there is dramatically less time for housework than there used to be. You have to let certain things go. And go. And go.

Household Tip #1:
Don't sweat the small stuff.

If you're like most people, you try to fit all your housework into a single weekend session. (Really makes you look forward to the weekend, doesn't it?) Or you try to stay awake long enough to clean the bathrooms after the kids are in bed for the night. Trust me, there are better ways.

Seize the Moment

Time management has a lot to do with how well you keep up with the house. If you try to schedule a huge block of time to do all those things you never get a chance to do, you'll wait a long time for that slot. Instead, you could make the most of those spare moments while Kendra is drying her hair or Roger is walking the dog. While you're waiting, pick up. Get the chicken out of the freezer for dinner. Do a quick refrigerator check and list the things you can pick up from the grocery on your way home. Learn to seize the moment and fit doable tasks into it, and you'll find yourself with less to schedule at the end of the day or week.

What kinds of things can you do in a spare moment or two? Pick up toys, open mail, read notes from teachers, put away dried dishes, plan dinner, fold socks, wipe a countertop, start a load of laundry, make a bed, open curtains, sweep a

floor, straighten a cabinet. If you have trouble
thinking of things you can do quickly, make a list
as they occur to you. Then, when you find
yourself standing at the door with your briefcase
waiting for Lauren to pack up her science project,
you can check the list and knock out one of the
items. One working mother of two does it this
way:

♦ ♦

*"Once every couple of days, I walk through the house
with a little notebook—something I can keep in my
pocket. I make a list of absolutely everything I see that
needs to be done. In the morning, before I leave for
work, I check the list to see if there's anything I can do.
At night, I check it again. All week long I work on that
list, and on Fridays I read back through it. I'm amazed
at the number of things I can cross off in a week's
time! It really makes me feel good to know I do all that I
do and I'm still able to accomplish that much at home."*

♦ ♦

What quick jobs can be done around your house to
lighten your "cleaning detail" later? Give some
serious thought to the things that drive you crazy
because you never seem to get to them. In my
house, that includes a loose drawer that needs to
be reglued, fingerprints on the door frames, a bowl
full of change I want to put into rolls, plants with
brown leaves begging to be removed, and probably
20 other things.

Make a list of simple tasks you can do in a "while-
you-wait" 10-minute period. Then put the list
somewhere easy to find—on the fridge, on the
bulletin board—and refer to it when you have a
moment to spare.

Sponsor a To-Do competition at your house. Show your kids the To-Do list, and give them a challenge: "Each time you do one of the To-Do chores, cross it off the list and initial it. At the end of the week, whoever has done the greatest number of chores wins." Be specific about what they will win, and about how and when they can collect. You might use allowance bonuses, special movies or privileges, or a long-awaited toy to give incentive to their efforts.

Do a Little at a Time

When it comes to things like keeping the house in tolerable order, you're best off doing a little at a time. Instead of letting things accumulate—not doing the laundry until Saturday, when you will have five loads to do—try to knock them out a little at a time. Do one load of laundry a day— every day, if you need to—and make sure it's washed, dried, and put away *that day*. Don't let it carry over until tomorrow. Then, in the morning, start again. You can start a load almost without thinking—maybe before you leave for work in the morning—then toss the clothes in the dryer later (like when you get home from work). Once you get yourself in the habit, it will almost seem like the laundry is doing itself. (And if you can get the kids to fold and put away, even better!)

One working father uses this spread-it-out approach with household repair projects:

"I work so many hours that I have trouble getting the time to work on the house. So I try to do one fix-it thing a night. Like the faucet dripping. Or putting oil on a squeaky door. I feel like I'm keeping up with things better if I don't let a lot of little things go."

What kinds of things can you manage a little at a time? Think of the things you spend a lot of time on—things you will be doing over and over, no matter what—not one-time projects, like painting the living room or hanging that shutter. Tasks that you do repeatedly will seem much more manageable if you tackle them frequently. Here are a few examples:

 Dishes. We all know the sinking feeling of walking into the kitchen after an exhausting day to face stacks of dirty dishes. Get into the habit of washing them right after you use them, and teach your family to be dish-responsible. They *can* learn to put a glass or dish in the dishwasher when they're finished with it. ("You use it, you load it.")

 Laundry. I'm not sure why laundry has such emotional control over me, but I've been known to stand helpless before piles of dirty clothes with thoughts like, "I just can't keep up. I'll never get this done. I should be a better housekeeper." If the laundry has you feeling powerless, stay on top of it. One load a day keeps that monster mound out of your basement (and may keep the kids from complaining about mismatched socks).

 General straightening. This one gets under my family's skin, but I'm a firm believer in staying on top of clutter. When you're finished in a particular room, make sure it's straight before you leave it. If it was straight when you went in, how much of a mess could you have made? Don't leave it for later, or you'll have to deal with it later. Do it now, clean and simple. Later, when you've got 14 other things to do, you'll be glad you did.

 Organizing bills. If only we could pay bills once and be done with it. But no, they keep coming, accumulating throughout the month until payday rolls around. To keep your stress level low and your coping level high, have a system to organize and pay your bills. As soon as you get the mail, every day, open it and file it in its proper place. This avoids the stack of bills that grows on the countertop (what a depressing sight!) and keeps you from accidentally misplacing something you really need to act on.

Household Tip #2:
Clean one room a day to avoid spending your whole weekend with the mop.

Who's Job Is It, Anyway?

I knew things had to change at my house when my then 5-year-old son Christopher (who had Napoleonic tendencies anyway) refused to pick up the pajamas he'd thrown on the floor, saying, "What do you think I am, the maid?"

Shocked but not silenced, I asked, "Who do you think the maid is?"

"You are," he said matter-of-factly.

After my blood pressure returned to normal, we established that (1) he didn't know what a maid was (he had heard the line on TV the night before) and (2) it was time to set some *Very Clear Rules About Who Does What Around Here.*

Here are the rules we came up with:

   If you got it out, put it back.

   If you're finished playing with it, put it away.

   If you wore it, hang it up.

   If you spilled it, clean it up.

If you broke it, admit it.

 If you'll help me, I'll help you.

After we established the rules, we had a long training period. In some families, this might be a "retraining" period. Maybe you established some guidelines early on about household responsibilities and now you need to clarify things a bit. But it does work, and it does help. And having the lines of responsibility drawn helps your kids know what's theirs to do and what isn't. When 15-year-old Adam tells 10-year-old Seth, "Make my bed," Seth glances up from his Batman game and says, "Make it yourself—it's *your* bed." Fair enough.

Household Tip #3:
Be willing to let things look less than perfect.

BEST & WORST

Best:
"Teaching children to handle responsibilities"

Organizing Household Tasks

Once you've establish the things you can do in spare moments and the things you can do a little at a time, you can start chipping away at the rest of the tasks you do on a regular basis. Setting up a system to organize household responsibilities may sound like a lot of effort for a little gain— who wants to spend even more time thinking about all the things you have trouble getting to? But in the time you ordinarily spend watching a rerun on TV (don't worry—it will be on again) you can make a schedule that will take a lot of the hassle and headache out of your household chores.

In the next section, you'll learn to identify areas where you need extra help around the house. The extra help might come in the form of chores your kids do or a new way to organize things to make your life easier.

When Does It Get Done?

One of the easiest ways to make sure things get done regularly is to create a housework schedule. Nothing fancy, just a written-down schedule of when the floor gets mopped, when the bathrooms are cleaned, when the sweeper is run, and the like. Once you write it all down, you can stop carrying it around in your head and maybe let yourself relax a while. Your housework schedule might look something like this:

Housework Schedule

To Do	How Often	When?
Clean bathrooms	Once a week	Saturday mornings
Run the sweeper	Twice a week	Tuesday & Friday evenings
Dust the furniture	Once a week	Saturday mornings
Mop the kitchen	Every two weeks	Saturday afternoon
Wipe fingerprints	Once a month	Saturday afternoon
Empty trash cans	Twice a week	Tuesday & Friday evenings

First make a list of all the chores to be done around (inside *and* outside) your house. Then determine how often they should be done. Finally, choose when they will fit into your family's schedule. Don't create the schedule thinking you'll do this all yourself. The idea is to enlist (or, if necessary, draft) other family members into sharing the wealth of work.

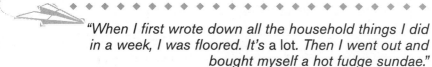

"When I first wrote down all the household things I did in a week, I was floored. It's a lot. Then I went out and bought myself a hot fudge sundae."
—Mother of one who works full-time

Household Tip #4:
Make housework easy on yourself.

Housework Schedule

To Do	How Often?	When?

What Do You Need?

Once you realize you need to try something new to get the house in shape, the question is, "What?"

There are several ways you can respond.

First, when you realize the grass is knee-high and you can only see the tips of bunny ears as they nibble your overgrown garden, ask yourself, "What do I need in order to fix this?" You'll probably hear a number of answers:

 Help!

 A teenager to mow the grass.

 Someone to weed the garden.

 More time so I can weed the garden.

 No garden, so I don't have to weed it.

 Artificial grass, so it doesn't need mowing.

 Cows to graze and keep the yard trimmed. (No, because then we'd need a fence, too.)

The first step in recovering from that overwhelmed feeling is recognizing you are overwhelmed. Then you can begin to think about ways to get the help you need.

Help might come in the form of other people. Maybe a neighbor could help you strip the wax off the kitchen floor (does anybody really do that anymore?) or get those impatiens planted before they wilt. Help might come in the form of time management. Maybe this is one of those things you could do a little at a time (even if you just mow a six-foot-square section of grass every day). Maybe it's something you could delegate to someone else, something you don't need to be doing yourself at all. Do you really have to pick up the dry-cleaning, even though it's 20 minutes out of your way? There might be other options, if you stop to think about them.

Household Tip #5:
Plan simple meals
for weeknights.

Let Yourself Think

The second step in determining what you need is to give yourself time to think about what would help. Do you need more time? More help? More resources? More options?

Look at the issue that's giving you trouble. Take the laundry. (Please!) If it's piling up, consider why. Get a piece of paper and write the problem at the top: "Why am I having trouble getting the laundry done?" Then write down the answers as they come to you:

1. There's too much of it.

2. I never have enough time to finish it.

3. Someone is always in the shower.

4. The washer is broken.

Within each of these answers are clues to how you can solve the problem. If there's too much laundry, ask yourself why. Are the kids throwing clean clothes in the basket? Are you trying to do it all at once instead of a little at a time? Is there another option you haven't let bubble up yet?

Go through your list, item by item, and write down any other questions, solutions, or options that come to you. Some answers will be obvious; others may surprise you. In any event, you won't be able to get the kind of help you need until you give yourself time to think of possible solutions.

"I've Always Done It This Way"

One answer you should *never* accept is, "We've always done it this way." If that's the best you can come up with, then it's probably time for a change.

Case in point: For 20 years, every time Diane made a roast beef, she cut the roast into two pieces and cooked them in separate pans. One day, her daughter asked her why she did that (thinking perhaps it made the meat more tender). Diane stopped and said, "I don't know. I've just always done it this way. My mother did it like this."

Intrigued, the daughter called Grandma, who laughingly explained that, when Diane was small, they had lived in a house with a tiny oven. In order to cook a roast big enough for the entire family, she'd had to divide it into two pans and fit them on separate shelves in the oven.

The moral? Whenever you find yourself saying, "I don't know—I've always done it like this," ask yourself whether it fits for you now.

Why am I having trouble with _____

1. _____
2. _____
3. _____
4. _____
5. _____

Ten Ways to Get the Help You Need

1. Have a clear picture of what you need help with.

2. Ask.

3. Be realistic about "when." If you have a situation you need to resolve *now*, do your best to take care of it quickly. But don't put unnecessary pressure on yourself when it's unwarranted.

4. Focus on one task and finish it before moving on to the next.

5. Be willing to be less than perfect. Don't feel bad that you can't finish everything. Reverse your thinking and celebrate because you finish something.

6. Use your resources. If friends or relatives offer help, accept it.

7. Let the people who offer help do it their way. Don't insist that the T-shirts be folded the way you've always done it. If they're folded, they're folded.

8. Focus on the most important things first. Take time to prioritize what you need to spend your time on. You can deal with the less important things later.

9. Don't rule out paid help. If you need a housekeeper, a professional organizer, a lawn service company, or a handyman—even if it's just a one-shot deal—admit it and get help. If it makes your life easier and it's worth the investment, go for it.

10. Think creatively about a solution; don't just settle for the first answer that comes to mind.

Household Tip #6:
Make sure you've got all the tools you need before you start a job.

Designing a Chore List

When you were coming up with your family priorities, mission statement, and rules, you probably listed who does what around the house. Perhaps your first question, when you noticed the grass overtaking the fire hydrant, was, "Who's job is it to mow the grass?"

What? You don't have a chore list? Oh, your kids are going to *love* this.[1] In fact, studies show that kids respond well to having things written out for them. They like to know what's expected of them, and they are more likely to meet—and exceed— your expectations when they have a good idea of what you want.

Like anything else, you should present the chore list in a family meeting with a "let's-make-this-family-work" kind of attitude. Everyone helps, everyone is important. The only time a chore list doesn't work is when it's uneven or unfair—that is, when one of the kids gets more work than the others, or when you assign all the jobs and don't do anything yourself (and how likely is *that*?)

Daily Chore List

Name: _____

_____

_____

_____

_____

Name: _____

_____

_____

_____

_____

Name: _____

_____

_____

_____

_____

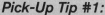

Pick-Up Tip #1:
Teach your toddler to put away
as part of the game you're playing.
Getting-out and putting-away are the
beginning and ending points of playing
with blocks, puzzles, crayons, trucks,
whatever. The earlier you start, the easier
it will be to enlist your child's help.

A few suggestions for creating a chore list:

 Bring up the idea at a family meeting.
Explain that you need help with the house
and you're looking for willing volunteers.
Explain that if you don't get willing
volunteers, you'll call in the draft. Ask each
child to come up with three chores he or she
would "like" to do each weekday (you may
want to give them weekends off or have
different Saturday chores). There may be
some haggling ("But I don't want to unload
the dishwasher! I want to feed the dog!"), but,
as much as possible, let the kids work out
who does what. It's your job to act as
secretary and write down the jobs they
finally agree to.

 Set a time limit for the chore roster. You
might say, for example, "Okay, we're going to
try this for a month. Cindy, you'll load the
dishwasher, bring in the mail, and set the
table every day for a month. Kyle, you feed
the dog, make sure the toys are picked up in
the family room, and put the clothes in the
laundry basket. At the end of the month,
we'll see if you want to trade jobs or chose
something else."

 **Include all kids, no matter what their
ages.** Everyone can do something. As soon
as Cameron is old enough to know a spoon
from a fork, he can help set the table. When

Lisa is home from college, she can still take the trash out on Monday nights.

Chore Possibilities

Pick up toys	Set the table
Fold laundry	Make the bed
Run the sweeper	Bring in the newspaper
Take out the trash	Bring in the trash cans
Dust furniture	Get the mail
Let the dog out	Feed pets
Water plants	Clip coupons
Make snacks	Weed the garden
Mow the lawn	Sweep the floors

Household Tip #7:
Don't answer the phone
while you're cleaning.

Teaching Kids About Chores

You may have "chore memories" from your childhood that still haunt you. What were your jobs around the house? I had to bring in the milk. Two glass bottles once a week, left in the stainless steel milkbox on the front porch. (Boy, that really dates me.) I also set the table for dinner, cleaned the upstairs bathroom on Saturdays, and dried dishes every night after supper. (My brother always got to wash. *I* always wanted to wash.)

Your kids learn important things from having chores at home. They learn about teamwork, responsibility, and cause-and-effect. They find out about family responsibility, which helps them grow into a bigger sense of societal and personal responsibility later.

Here are some tips for teaching your children about chores:

 Make it matter-of-fact. Treat the chores as a part of life, not something to be negotiated or candy-coated. The attitude should be, "We all have a part to play, and this is yours." Give the role the respect it deserves: You need each and every member of your household pulling together to make things work. Zach might be helping with little things now, but in a year or two, he'll be able to do much bigger things by himself because you've helped him learn to handle responsibility early.

 Expect grumbling. Who among us would fold laundry if we could whine a little and have someone else do it for us? Don't be shocked, dismayed, or angered when your kids grumble. They will. Just fall back on the matter-of-fact attitude and explain that chores go with the territory.

 Reward performance. Set up a system to reward your kids (and yourself) when they accomplish the goals you've set together. You may want to start allowances, if you haven't already done that. Or use other incentives, like special freedoms, trips to concerts, family excursions, or sleep-over privileges. To encourage team spirit, you could set a family goal: "When we have a week when we all get our chores done without reminders, we'll go to the movies."

Chore Incentive Programs

How you encourage your kids to complete their chores is, of course, up to you. You might simply insist that chores be completed before a favorite activity is allowed:

◆ ◆

"Ryan, your bed must be made before you can play video games."

"Maggie, your chores must be finished before you can talk on the phone."

◆ ◆

You might want to use an allowance as a motivational factor. If your children perform their chores without any prompting from you for five consecutive days, what's it worth to you? Some parents are comfortable with that. Others feel that chores are simply part of family responsibilities, and that kids should do them without expecting compensation.

A mother of three who works full-time put it this way:

◆ ◆

"I started out paying my son Chad for the chores he did, but all of a sudden, every time I saw him, he had his hand out. He'd say. 'Mom, I brought in the trash can for you,' and hold out his hand. Or 'Mom, I let the dog out,' and that hand would go out. I started feeling like he thought I was supposed to pay him for every nice thing he did. So I made a list of 10 things and said, 'These are the things I'll pay you for. Everything else you do is just because you're such a great kid.'"

◆ ◆

Whatever your feelings on the subject, you're going to get better results if you reward your children for doing their jobs. Whether that reward is a simple acknowledgment ("Jason, your bed looks great!"), a hug or compliment, a special treat, or some other way you think to say "Good job," letting your children know that you notice and appreciate their help is an important part of making sure they continue it.

At our house, the old gold-stars-on-the-chart idea worked well for several weeks, until the baby got hold of the stars and stuck them everywhere—on the television, the stereo, the couch, the dog. A simple checklist—or better, a page where kids can add stickers each day they complete their chores—gives you (and them) a visual record of how well they are doing. Hang the chart in your family information area so everyone can see how hard they are working.

Household Tip #8:
When the family helps, let them do it their way—and be appreciative.

Tipping the Allowance Scales

If you decide to go the allowance route, how do you know the going rate? (Better not ask your kids what their friends are getting. You may hear a slightly exaggerated "average.") Should you dole it out a quarter at a time, or make it a lump sum at the end of the week? Should it be tied completely to chores ("If you don't do your chores, you don't get paid"), or should it be given simply on merit? Lots of questions that only you can answer.

Experts suggest, however, that the primary reason to give an allowance is to help your children learn about money, not to coerce their cooperation in family chores. In *Family Rules*, Dr. Kenneth Kaye suggests you protect a portion of the allowance that is irrevocable—in other words, your kids get a certain part of their allowance even if they don't do their chores.[2]

You can make some of the allowance contingent on the completion of chores: This sets up a natural consequence that you can enforce easily and will encourage your children to do their chores. For example, you might tell Jill she loses 50 cents of her allowance each time she forgets to put the dishes in the dishwasher. After a few shortages, she might start remembering the dishes.

So, how much should you pay? The ages of your children have a lot to do with it. Older children might need extra money for things like bus fare or school lunches; younger children need little money in order to learn the spending and responsibility lessons an allowance can teach. Many parents of teenagers feel that kids shouldn't receive an allowance at all—that any spending money above and beyond school expenses the teenager should earn him- or herself, by doing extra chores, mowing lawns, shoveling snow, baby-sitting, or getting an after-school job.

When you know the allowance thing isn't working

A teenager was asked what she does to earn the $10 allowance she gets every week. She looked at the questioner, dumbfounded. "What do you mean, 'What do I *do*?'"

Generally, $1 to $2 a week is more than enough for elementary school children. (Remember, you might want to make one part of the allowance contingent on chores and one part irrevocable.) For junior high students, you might go up a few dollars—to $4 or $5—especially if the student is paying bus fare. High school opens up yet more options, with off-campus lunches, flower sales, candy sales, and other miscellaneous ways your teen will want to spend money. Again, decide for yourself how you feel most comfortable handling the allowance issue and then make the information available to the kids. Another family meeting? You bet.

They'll want to know why some of the kids are "making more" than others. Have your explanations ready. And remember that the most important thing an allowance does is help your child learn how to make money decisions—both how to work for it and how to spend it. Using it solely as something to take away when they don't do their chores teaches them only the effects of irresponsibility, not the rewards of responsibility.

Daily Chore Record

Name: _____

Monday: _____

Tuesday: _____

Wednesday: _____

Thursday: _____

Friday: _____

Pick-Up Tip #2:
Choose a "clean up song" that you play whenever it's time to clean up. Give your preschoolers a five-minute warning ("Okay guys, when I put the song on, you need to start cleaning up."), then put the song on. The song reminds them and gives them something pleasant to sing along with. The room gets clean, and there's no nagging or frustration for you.

Household Tip #9:
Don't redo what others
have already done.

Recipe for Harmonious Housework

1 chore list	2 (or more) willing helpers
1 housework schedule	a good serving of patience
resolve to keep trying	realistic expectations
a sense of humor	encouraging words

Gather all ingredients in any order; mix well. Add a heavy sprinkling of encouraging words and keep trying, week after week, until you get it right.

Streamlining Household Efforts

Throughout this section, you've explored different ways to solve some of the issues piling up around you. You can deal with quick things in spare moments. You can spread big jobs out and do a little at a time. You can delegate chores so that everybody is helping.

Something else to think about is streamlining your efforts. By organizing tasks, you can do all of one type at once, thereby lessening the time and effort they require. Case in point: Changing the bedsheets. If you're the one changing all the sheets, do them all at once, every bed, every room. Don't start to strip Brian's bed, then pick up his toys (he should be doing that anyway!), fold his clothes, straighten his closet, and so on. Focus on that one thing and knock it out—for every room in which it applies.

Or you might do all the bathrooms in one fell swoop. You've got the toilet brush, your gloves, the glass cleaner, whatever—now do all the bathrooms at once, while you're in "bathroom mode." When you dust, dust everything. When you sweep, sweep all the floors that need it. Then you'll know you're done, completely, with that task.

Here are a few other time-saving tips for household chores:

 Plan what you're going to tackle before you tackle it. Make sure you've got the tools you need—a mop, the floor wax, a bucket, whatever—before you begin.

 Write out a calendar that shows when you do different tasks. Maybe you mop the downstairs once every two weeks, vacuum the living room twice a week, wipe fingerprints once a month, do windows— when?

Housework Calendar

SUNDAY	MONDAY	TUESDAY	WEDNESDAY	THURSDAY	FRIDAY	SATURDAY
1	2	3	4	5	6	7
8	9	10	11	12	13	14
15	16	17	18	19	20	21
22	23	24	25	26	27	28
29	30	31				

Errands, Errands, Everywhere

How much time do you spend in the car, driving to this store and that, stopping at the post office, running by the bank? With a little forethought, you can organize your errands into stops you can make after work or perhaps on your lunch hour. (Don't try to do them before work unless you're really comfortable with the cushion of time you have in the morning.) Think about what errands fall along your route, when you absolutely need to do them, and what the priorities are. This saves you from running all over town when you'd really rather be home with your family.

Here are a few additional tips to make your errand-running easier:

 Don't do on foot what you can do by phone. If you can accomplish your goals by calling, try that first. It may save you a trip.

 Organize all your errands into a single trip. Think about where you need to go and hit the places in a logical progression.

 Make sure you have everything you need before you leave. If you decide to run an errand on your lunch hour, be sure you've got the sales receipt, the laundry ticket, whatever. (You may want to put these items in the glove compartment of your car so you've always got them.)

 Assemble all the things you need to deliver on your errands in your going-

out place: books going back to the library, laundry to the cleaners, a shirt back to the store, whatever.

Organizing Is Worth the Effort

Many people have mental blocks about organizing. We remember grade-school teachers frowning down at us and saying, "You need to get yourself organized!" More recently, college professors—or perhaps bosses—may have noticed (with displeasure) our avant-garde approach to project management.

What's wrong with being organized?

Some of us think being organized—*really* organized, so we know roughly the balance of our checkbooks and where our car keys are, are sure that our briefcase is where we left it, and have a sense of where each of our children is at this very moment—means being restricted. No freedom. A regimented lifestyle.

But, as Pipi Campbell Peterson points out, "*realistically* planning allows us *more* freedom."[3] When we get organized, we spend less time in a wild panic looking for things we needed 20 minutes ago. We stop moving piles of things from place to place and put them where they go—once and for all. We simply *maintain* the organization once we've created it, which certainly takes a lot less work than dealing with chaos.

If you're a good sorter, you can organize. It's simply a matter of thinking about what goes where and then doing it. The thinking is the key part.

Do You Need to Organize?

We all have different mess-tolerance levels. Plastic building blocks scattered over the family room carpet might not bother you, but (for more than an hour at a time) they bother me—especially in bare feet! I probably won't notice fingerprints on the windows, but they might drive you crazy.

On a larger scale, you might have a well-designed system for paying bills, getting your car serviced, keeping up with home improvements, and so on. I might just sit here and pray nothing happens that will force me to go hunting for a warranty agreement I know I'll never find.

The level of organization you need to keep your home running smoothly depends on your lifestyle and the needs of your family. Generally, the more complicated your life, the more you need to be organized. There are exceptions, however. Some people write everything down—from the time they intend to call their mother to what they need to thaw for dinner next Tuesday night. Others try to keep everything in their heads—usually with more than a couple of oversights, no matter how good their memories.

 When you find yourself trying to remember too much—this appointment, that password, your deadline, his phone number, her shoe size—start writing things down. Invest 39 cents and get yourself a pocket notebook. When those little bits of information start cluttering your thoughts, write them down and get them off your mind. Your brain will thank you for it.

You know you need to organize things at home when ...

 You leave the house late more than three days in a row.

You can't find socks that match.

 You are looking for a legal document and there are several places it "could be."

 You are always searching for phone numbers on scraps of paper that were "right there a minute ago."

 You spend 10 minutes searching through clothes that don't fit anymore to locate something that does.

 You still have shoes from the '70s.

 You feel you have to know when someone is "stopping by" so you can do a whirlwind clean-up before they arrive.

 You look around at the clutter and feel overwhelmed.

One mother of four, an executive secretary who works 30 hours a week, explained her introduction to organization this way:

"It wasn't until everything started falling apart that I realized, in a panic, that there must be a better way to get things done around the house. We were at each other's throats all the time—each of us blaming the others for everything being a mess, not being able to find the things we needed, etc. So we gave each person a room: Each child is responsible for keeping his or her room clean and has one other room besides. Elizabeth straightens the kitchen and her room; Brandon picks up the living room and his room; Sara is in charge of the bathrooms and her room; and Scott, the youngest, takes care of the dining room (all he has to do is set the table for dinner) and his bedroom. On the weekends, we do the big cleaning, but the house basically stays straight through the week. And if it doesn't, we know whose name to call!"

Where Do You Need to Organize?

Most of us are pretty-well organized in some areas of our lives and not-so-organized in others. You might do a great job organizing your bills, for example, but not have a clue where your appliance manuals and warranties are. Or perhaps you've got laundry down to a science (one load a day, begun in the morning, finished in the evening), but things like storage—what to keep and where to keep it—leave you helpless.

 If you don't have a system for organizing bills and other household papers, see "A Filing System" later in this chapter.

While you're still in the thinking-about-organizing stage, walk around the house with a notebook and do a pre-organizing tour. Make a note of any room, corner, or shelf that is disorganized. You won't necessarily organize all the items you see—and you certainly won't do them all right now—but it will give you an idea of where to begin.

The Pre-Organizing Tour

These places need to be organized:

_____

_____

_____

_____

_____

_____

_____

_____

_____

_____

BEST &
WORST

Worst:
"By the
time I get
home from
work, feed
the family,
get the
children
bathed and
read to, and
finish
household
chores,
there is
no time left
for me to do
anything but
sleep."

Planning the Attack

If organizing the house ultimately falls on your shoulders, it behooves you to think about how you can best approach the task. The job may seem formidable, depending on how large a space you've got to arrange and how many other things you've got going on at the same time.

Here are a few guidelines to help you stay grounded in reality:

 Don't expect to get everything done in one afternoon, or even one weekend. If you are organizing files, boxes, closets, rooms, basements, and attics, plan on making "organizing" your new hobby for the next several weeks. Think of it as an extended spring cleaning session. But once you're finished, you'll only need to maintain the organization you've established. Getting organized is the most difficult part—then it's just a matter of *staying* organized.

 As soon as you get started, the kids will want to help. And if your kids are like mine, "helping" means "going through these boxes to see if there's anything I want." So 8-year-old Christopher tries to sneak out of the room with an AM radio that hasn't worked in 12 years. "Where are you going with that?" I ask. "I'm gonna' do something with it," he says. Do something with it. That means it will end up in *his* pile of junk, which I'll no doubt be sorting through sometime before the start of the next millennium.

 Careful thought now will keep you on track later. Once you begin organizing, the pull to get sidetracked will be great. You'll discover old memories and new mementos and find things you forgot to resolve years ago. Decide before you begin what it is you want to accomplish in that 30-minute, or 2-hour, or all-afternoon cleaning session. Say your goal out loud. "Before I leave this room, I'm going to finish that filing cabinet." Then stick to it.

Kits for Making Housework Easier

Especially if you delegate jobs to your kids, you can make housecleaning a lot easier by putting together cleaning "kits" that include all the things needed for different jobs. Then, when you say, "John, clean up the soda you just spilled on the carpet," John can go to the cleaning closet (it helps to keep all the cleaning supplies together so you don't hear the inevitable, "I can't find it!"), get the cleaning kit he needs (in this case, the carpet care kit), and get to work. Here are a few kits you could easily create from things you've probably already got around the house:

- Mopping kit: mop, bucket, and floor cleaner

- Dusting kit: spray or oil, duster or cloths

- Spills kit: a roll of paper towels, sponge, small container for water

- Carpet care kit: carpet spot cleaner, a scrub brush, sponge, small container

- Bathroom cleaning kit: sink and tub cleaner, toilet cleaner, gloves, a sponge, toilet brush[4]

Even if you don't organize the items into kits, make sure you have cleaning supplies on hand for routine and emergency jobs. And, if you've got the space, put all the supplies together in one place—this lets you keep an eye on your inventory.

Once you get your cleaning closet organized, take the kids on a tour. Show them what's in there, how they will use the supplies, which supplies *not* to use, and what to do when spills happen, when the dog doesn't make it to the door, when it's their turn to clean the sink in the basement. Take 15 minutes to dole out useful information now, and you may save an hour's worth of consternation later in the week.

Setting Realistic Expectations

Before you start setting goals for yourself, make sure you're thinking realistically. In fact, if you're just beginning to get organized, give yourself the benefit of the doubt and set simple goals. Then, when you meet them, reward yourself. Pat yourself on the back.

If you set your goals too high ("I'm going to get this entire basement organized while the baby sleeps!"), you're setting yourself up for failure. Take it slow and easy. Remember, any organizing is a step in the right direction. You're improving your system, no matter how slowly it seems to be going.

What are realistic expectations?

 For a start, just *think* about organizing your house. Write down a few notes, if you want, but give yourself time to consider what you want to change, how you want it changed, what might make it better, what tools you need, and so on. Then set a date to begin the actual organizing.

 Do one thing the first day. Organize the junk drawer. (That may not be starting small enough, if your junk drawer is like mine.) Or refold all the towels and separate them from the tablecloths in the linen closet.

 Keep a list. Make a list of all the organizing you need to do. When you finish a task, take a break, cross the item off the list, and celebrate a little.

 Prioritize the jobs. Make sure the tasks you tackle first are the ones that will bring you the biggest benefit. For example, you might want to create your family information center or your going-out place first, because those two items help your whole family stay in step.

Organizing Priorities

These places need to be organized in this order:

_____

_____

_____

_____

_____

_____

_____

_____

_____

_____

Pipi Campbell Peterson's *Ready, Set, Organize!* is a wonderful workbook that leads you through the process of organizing your entire household system. From basic time management to step-by-step organization of stored items, clothing, papers, and important records, *Ready, Set, Organize!* gives you a road map through—and out of—clutter forever.[5]

Where Should You Start?

Considering all the changes your family is going through and the balancing act you're learning, you should start wherever it will save you the most time. If you hardly ever go into the basement, don't spend your time and effort there. You may want to start with the family information center we talked about in chapter 1.

The Family Information Center

Some families set up their information center on the refrigerator; others create a bulletin board somewhere close to the telephone or in a central area everyone is likely to see. Include these items in your family information center:

 A large monthly calendar with write-in spaces to record all family activities.

 A set of colored markers, so each family member can have his or her own color.

 A list of important phone numbers, including Mom's and Dad's work numbers; the police, fire, and poison control centers; the baby-sitter's; the school; any after-school clubs; and close neighbors.

Phone numbers of your children's friends, organized by child.

 A pad of paper for "we-need-this-from-the-grocery" items.

 Post-It notes for questions. ("Mom, can I go to Sara's house after school on Thursday?")

 Push-pins for important notices and school permission slips.

 Phone message pads.

Make sure each person in your family old enough to read and write understands the importance of updating his or her own information on the board. If Grant's game is moved from Tuesday to Monday, he needs to change it on the board (and hopefully tell you, too). If someone calls for you during the afternoon and Carrie takes a message, she should write the name, number, and message on the message pad and pin it where you'll see it.

Each night when you get home from work, check the information center to see what has changed. You might want to make a nightly habit of asking if anyone has changes to make (the dinner table is a good place to catch everyone together). The board won't work unless you stay current. With just a few minutes' attention each night, it can dramatically simplify the day-to-day operation of your family.

The Going-Out Place

Another way to help smooth the rough spots is to set up a going-out place. We discussed this in chapter 3, when getting out the door on time was presenting such a challenge.

A going-out place is a spot—usually by the front or back door—where you put all the items you need to grab on your way out. This might include your briefcase, lunches, bookbags, snow boots, car keys, and other necessary tools for the day.

Consider what items your family needs in a going-out place before you choose the site. At our house, we need room for snow boots, bookbags, and extra things like homework projects and swimming bags. Because of the snow boots, we use a heavy-duty floor mat to mark the "place." The bookbags, boots, and other items fit nicely on the 2'-by-3' mat, and it's placed right by the door. The kids just scoop up what they need on their way out to the bus.

Your going-out place might include things like coat and hat hooks, a small basket for keys, a bulletin board for last-minute notes, and/or an umbrella stand. You can probably come up with other items unique to the accessories your family uses.

The trick to the going-out place is using it consistently. With the family information center, you need to keep it updated in order for it to work; with the going-out place, you have to faithfully put everything in its place the night before you need it. Bookbags, boots, and other items should be right there, by the door, before bed the night before. That way, in the morning your out-the-door exit can happen in one smooth motion.

A Filing System

Another mess gathers on the countertops of America: piles of bills and stray papers. Even in this day of ecological consciousness, we receive mounds and mounds of papers—catalogs, bills, letters from friends and companies—and they tend to accumulate on counters and tables, in drawers, or on shelves until we devise some means of dealing with them. Part of "digging out" of household chaos is organizing and filing the papers that are so much a part of our lives.

◆ ◆

*"My daughter and I were going around about
her grades. 'You're just too disorganized,' I said.
'If you'd get your assignments organized, you'd get
better grades.' She sighed and asked me what I'd done
with her report card. I looked over at the stack of
papers on the counter. 'Oh, I don't know,' I said. 'It's
somewhere in that mess.'"*
—Mother of two who works full-time

◆ ◆

What Do You Need to File?

If you've been running a household for any length
of time, you know how important it is to be able to
find things when you need them. Certain papers
you need access to quickly; others you can file
away and forget, digging them out only if
necessary. Generally, you'll need to create a filing
system that helps you organize documents in
these categories:

 Family: You need to store birth certificates,
immunization records, school records, day-
care information, Social Security
information, wills, report cards, passports,
and other important documents. Don't forget
space for special drawings and paintings,
names and numbers of back-up sitters, photo
IDs, fingerprint records, and pertinent health
information and policies.

 Household: You've got bills to track and
store and financial information to keep,
including investments, bank statements, tax
returns, retirement policies, life insurance
information; and information on your house,
appliances, inventory, and improvements.

 Vehicles: You need to store information on
car payments, insurance cards and policies,
repair schedules and receipts, and other
necessary information.

You need files for legal papers, for medical papers, for information on each of your children. You need files for your bills, preferably sorted according to creditor and organized with some kind of bill-paying calendar. You need someplace to put bills until they are paid, and someplace to put the bill receipts after they are paid. Many people use file folders or accordion files to store these kinds of things. You may want to invest in a filing cabinet and hanging file folders, depending on how much you have to organize.

Show your kids what you're doing—introduce them to your filing system. Let them see that the effort you expend now will save you considerable time and frustration you might otherwise spend looking for misplaced papers.

One mother puts her 7-year-old to work:

"When I have a number of things to file, like right after I pay bills, I have Brock be my assistant. He finds the file the electric bill goes in, for example, and puts the bill receipt away. I pay him 50 cents each time he does it, and he feels like he's done a 'job.' Plus, he's learned about filing papers and getting organized."
—Mother of one who works part-time

Make sure you've got a folder with information about your day-care arrangements, health care, insurance numbers, emergency procedures, and other important information you may need to access quickly. Show your kids where important papers are in case of an emergency, so they can get to any information they need that is not already posted on your family bulletin board.

Keeping Things Straight

Once you get hold of your household system and begin to get organized, how can you ensure that things keep running smoothly? The best possible tool you can use to ensure that life will continue on the upswing is praise. Remember to recognize your family's efforts. Remind them of how well they—and you—are doing. Focus on the teamwork, and reward success.

Especially at first, take failures in stride. People are going to forget—and perhaps flat-out rebel against—the new system. Whenever possible, focus on the positive and you'll get more of it.

Once a week, perhaps on Friday evenings, sit down with your spouse and review the week. What got done and what didn't? Did you wind up meeting more goals than you missed? Discuss what worked well this week and what you might want to change for next week.

Once a month—or sooner if something isn't working smoothly and you think a change is needed—sit down in a family meeting and discuss how things are going. How does the family feel about the system in place? Make sure the discussion is open and honest. Even if you hear considerable grumbling and griping, try to hear what's really being said. Be open to alternatives suggested by other family members. If the suggestion sounds like it might work, try it. (You can vote on it first.) The great thing about establishing a family system is that, once it's established, you can change it easily. Developing a system that works is a process that will grow and change as long as your family does.

Summary

In this chapter, you learned some practical techniques for getting your house and yard back under control. Especially when your priorities change and additional demands are made on your time, things around the house can slip into disarray. Tasks that were once easy to accomplish now regularly get the quick once-over, and you hope your guests won't notice. That's to be expected, especially at first. But with a little help and a few organizational skills, you can get things back under control—and functioning better than ever—in no time.

And once you've gotten the house back in some semblance of order, you're ready to sit back and breathe a little. Chapter 8 helps you protect your most valuable resource during this important time of change: *you.*

Notes

1. Actually, your kids may love it. Different personalities respond to things differently: My 14-year-old looks on most rules as personal affronts to her civil liberties, but my 8-year-old loves having things to do and "check off." And my 2-year-old loves to help, as long as I let him do it "his way," which is often a dangerous endeavor.

2. Kenneth Kaye, *Family Rules* (New York: St. Martins, 1984).

3. Pipi Campbell Peterson, *Ready, Set, Organize!* (Indianapolis: Park Avenue, 1996).

4. Kits that contain caustic or poisonous items— such as toilet cleaner or carpet spot remover— should obviously be kept out of reach of young children.

5. Peterson, *Ready, Set, Organize!*

Chapter

8

Time for You

"No day is so bad it can't be fixed with a nap."
—Carrie Snow

In the Rob Reiner movie *Parenthood*, the main character says to his wife in a moment of exasperation, "My whole *life* is have to!" If you're a working parent, you know what that means. From the time the alarm goes off in the morning to the precious few moments of silence at the end of the day (if you're still awake to hear them), your life is full of things to think about, plan, solve, orchestrate, and troubleshoot.

Especially in the transitional period when you first return to work, the temptation is great to take care of everyone and everything else first. You want to make sure the kids are okay. You're trying to get the house under control. You're looking for time to spend with your spouse.

But what about you?

Research shows that the more demands we have on our time, the more we need time to ourselves. We need to recuperate, relax, rest. Silence is a rare find of unquestionable medicinal value.

It is possible to find time for ourselves, even in the midst of transition, even in the center of stressful lives. We must make stress-busting a priority, however. Stress, in large doses or small, affects the way we see each other and ourselves. It also can dampen our spirits, make us jumpy or irritable, hamper our ability to make sound decisions with confidence, and generally affect our work performance. Stress, over the long haul, can add to your chances of physical damage, as well—from headaches to high blood pressure to heart attacks.

From One Parent to Another

"Sometimes when I'm feeling really stressed, I take a detour on my way home from work. I drive out in the country where nobody can hear me or see me, pull over to the side of the road, and scream as loud as I can. Usually I laugh at myself afterward, but I sure do feel better."
—Mother of three who works full-time

Stress? What Stress?

Some of us are so busy that we don't even notice the stress we're under. Statistics show that 30 percent of working Americans experience what they consider "high stress" nearly every day. The percentage is even higher for people who say they feel acute stress once or twice a week.

What does "high stress" feel like?

 The moment of panic when you realize the boss is going to ask for your report and it's not finished.

 The knot of anxiety you feel when you're facing a new computer program for the first time.

 The sick-to-your-stomach upset that hangs on after you leave your daughter at day care.

 The tightness in your neck and shoulders when you're stuck in traffic and late for an important meeting.

Your reaction to stress may be to play it down. After all, everyone lives with a certain amount of stress. But in recent years research has shown that stress affects our systems in very negative ways.

When you are under stress—whether it's acute or prolonged stress—your body overproduces adrenaline and other powerful hormones. This, in turn, suppresses the production of T-cells, which are an important part of your immune system.

The result? More colds. More flu. Lower resistance.

There are several things you can do to reduce your stress level and steps you can take toward setting up a self-care system so you don't end up down for the count.

◆ ◆ ◆ ◆ ◆ ◆ ◆ ◆ ◆ ◆ ◆ ◆ ◆ ◆ ◆ ◆ ◆ ◆ ◆ ◆

"When I know I'm under a lot of stress, I try to make sure to eat right and take vitamins. Even though I might be having trouble at work, it won't be compounded by me getting sick."
—Father of one who works full-time

◆ ◆ ◆ ◆ ◆ ◆ ◆ ◆ ◆ ◆ ◆ ◆ ◆ ◆ ◆ ◆ ◆ ◆ ◆ ◆

Three Keys to Lessening Stress

No matter what your daily routine is like, you're bound to deal with stress. Starting a new job is stressful. Raising kids is stressful. Life in the '90s is stressful.

How you respond to that stress is something you decide for yourself. Some people can see stress coming and neatly side-step it; others get steamrolled by it. Most of us fall somewhere in between. But with a little bit of observation, you can figure out what kinds of things stress you most and anticipate, avoid, or at least respond differently to those stresses in the future.

Key #1: Know What Stresses You Out

Before you can really begin to reduce the stress in your life, or consider ways to deal with it better, you must be able to recognize it. What really stresses you out? Talking about money? Giving presentations to the board? Helping the kids with their homework? Getting dinner on the table? We're all different, and what causes me a lot of anxiety might be laughably easy for you. Figure out what sets you off and, the next time the situation comes up, you'll be ready for it.

A major step in lessening stress is to put a real face on it. Being stressed out about the part of your job that will involve giving presentations before the management group is abstract—a kind of in-the-future fear. As a general situation, you can't solve that stress in one fell swoop. The questions Where? When? How? aren't answered.

You're not sure when you will have to give a presentation, where, how, or to whom—but it's stressing you. If you are dealing with this kind of abstract stress, resolve not to worry about it until it's a real event. Give yourself permission to start stressing out when they schedule your first presentation.

If you're anxious about the presentation you have to give next Tuesday, on the other hand, you can put a definite face on the stress. Now it's a real event. *That* you can do something about. You can practice, plan, study, prepare. You can pray that they cancel the meeting. You can make sure your presentation is so unbelievably good that it will knock their socks off. In any case, putting a real face on the stress allows you to take action to resolve it. Being fearful or stressed about a vague circumstance can do nothing but haunt you, until you deal with it in the concrete.

What Stresses You Out?

Here's your chance to make a list of your stressors (and check it twice):

This Stresses Me Out	Abstract or Concrete?
_____	_____
_____	_____
_____	_____
_____	_____
_____	_____
_____	_____

Key #2: Can You Change the Situation?

Some stressful situations you simply have to live with. Your brother-in-law has moved in while he's looking for a job and, well, you're stuck with him till the first of the month. Or you've got to find a fill-in baby-sitter for three days while your regular sitter is out of town. Or you prepared a spreadsheet based on erroneous figures they gave you in accounting, and there's nothing you can do about it now. When your stress is something you can't do anything about, you need to be able to let it go. The only healthy answer is to modify the way you react to the situation.

Look through your list and ask yourself if there is anything you can do about the stress. Stressed about finding the back-up baby-sitter? There are things you can do about that: Ask your current baby-sitter if she can recommend someone; check with area day cares to see if any of them has a drop-in policy; ask your mother if she can help out for those few days.

If the situation is something you can't change, do what you can to take care of yourself in spite of it. Here are a few ideas to help when you're experiencing a stressful situation that you can't change:

 Turn your thoughts to something else — preferably something pleasant.

 Take three or four deep breaths.

 If you can, get outside and go for a walk.

 Change your focus. If you're preparing for a meeting, stop and make a few phone calls or make those copies you were putting off. If you're trying to get the laundry done, put everything down and read your 2-year-old the story she's been wanting to hear.

 Meditate or pray.

Look at the pictures your kids made for your office.

 Listen to music that calms and soothes you.

Whatever your situation—whether the stress happens most at work or at home—you can change the way it affects you, even if you can't completely eliminate it. As you begin reducing the amount of stress you live with on a daily basis, you'll get accustomed to treating yourself better, which results in even less stress. It's a win-win cycle, and all you have to do is ask yourself about the things that stress you and determine to do whatever you can about them.

I grew up hearing the Serenity Prayer but didn't really understand it—or put it into practice—until I was an adult:

> *"God, grant me the serenity*
>
> *to accept the things I cannot change,*
>
> *the courage to change the things I can,*
>
> *and the wisdom to know the difference."*

Key #3: Take Action

The greatest stress hits us when we feel powerless. Taking action helps us feel back in control, which propels us forward and keeps us from getting stuck in the circumstance.

If you determine that the situation causing you stress is something you can do something about, the next question is, "What?" If you've put a face on the stress and see it as a concrete situation, you can brainstorm possible solutions.

Brainstorming is an easy way to find solutions to stressful situations. Look back at the list of things that cause you stress. Pick the one that causes the most anxiety and write it at the top of a sheet of paper. For example, you might write, "The drive home from work really stresses me out." Then turn the issue into a question: "What can I do to make the drive home less stressful?" Sit back and let the sparks fly. Write down every potential solution that comes to mind—no matter how far-fetched—for the next 5 or 10 minutes. Your list might look something like this:

The drive home really stresses me out.

What can I do to make the drive less stressful?

1. Leave earlier to avoid the traffic
2. Ask Carol if I can carpool with her.
3. Have Dan pick up the kids so I won't be in such a rush.
4. Try a new route home.
5. Get a new car so I'll enjoy the ride.
6. Take my Kenny G. tapes to soothe my nerves.
7. Take the bus.

You may or may not find the perfect answer in your first brainstorming session, but taking action is the key. You begin thinking creatively about how you can reduce your stress, which will eventually translate into a healthier, happier you.

Stress Busters

- Slow down.
- Take deep breaths.
- Meditate.
- Exercise.
- Visualize the situation being resolved the way you want it to be.
- Ask yourself what the situation is teaching you.
- Get outside if you can.

Taming the Dinnertime Crazies

Ask any group of working parents what the most stressful time of day is, and you'll get a surprisingly consistent answer: "arsenic hour," that 60-minute span of eternity that stretches from the time you walk in the door after work to the time everyone sits down to dinner. You may have it better or worse, depending on whether you cook the meals, how many kids you've got (and what their ages are), and whether your spouse shares equally in the pre-dinner challenge.

Why is this time so difficult? Most parents report that they feel pulled in several directions at once. The kids want to tell you all about their days, the dog needs to go out, you're trying to get dinner together, and the phone is ringing off the hook. Mix this with a work project that's hanging on in the back of your mind and a spouse who wants to talk about this weekend's plans, and you're headed for stress overload.

One mother solved this situation by stating forcefully what she needed:

"I'd walk in the door after being on my feet for 10 hours, knowing it would be at least another hour before I could sit down. That bothered me more and more, until I finally told my family, 'We're eating at 7:00, so I can sit down and rest a few minutes before I make dinner. If that's a problem for any of you, you can do the cooking.' Nobody complained, and now I come home, change clothes, and cuddle with the kids on the couch for a few minutes before I start dinner. Our evenings are completely different, and more often than not, the kids help me make and serve the meal. They never did that before."
—Mother of four who works full-time

Lightening the Lunacy

Here are a few ways you can tone down your first hour at home:

Leave work at work. Even if you commute and have time to review work issues on the way home, don't. Use the drive time to let your workday go and make the mental shift to "person, parent, spouse."

Know what you're walking into. Don't be surprised, day after day, by the frenzied pace of your household in that first hour home. Before it begins, prepare yourself for it. In some cases, a little clear communication can help. "Kevin, when I first get home from work, I really need a few minutes of quiet. Just let me change clothes and wash my face. Then I'd really like to hear all about your day."

Cut yourself some slack. If you need quiet, ask for it. Let the answering machine get the phone for the first hour. You can answer calls later, when you're not trying to do so much. You can reduce your expectations of yourself in other areas too. Don't try to make gourmet meals on weeknights; dishes don't *have* to be done the minute dinner is over. Sit at the table a few minutes after the kids excuse themselves and talk to your spouse. You'll both feel better for it.

 Look for the good. Resolve that the first thing you say to each child is something positive. "What a great art paper!" Or "You really did a good job picking out your clothes today." It's easy to walk in and see all the things that haven't been done, but the tone of the night—and your own internal stress level—will be better if you affirm rather than attack.

 Grab a few minute's peace. Yes, it's possible—even if it's just while you change your clothes or wash your face. Take a few minutes, slow down your pace, refresh yourself, change into something comfortable, and head out to face the troops as Mom or Dad.

 Remember that there's plenty of time for togetherness. No law says you must have family togetherness time while you're trying to fix dinner, answer phone messages, feed the dog, and look at the mail. Chances are, you're tired, the kids are tired (and probably hungry and grumpy too), and this may not be the most harmonious time for family interplay. If your kids are scattered all over the house doing their own things, let them amuse themselves until dinner. Encourage it with, "I love how you're taking care of yourselves. I can get dinner faster this way." After some alone time, dinnertime might be more peaceful.

BEST & WORST

Best: "Getting out of the house, meeting new people. My job allows me to work with children— which I love."

Kitchen Catch-Ups

Throughout this book, you've no doubt picked up on the theme that organizing makes life easier. Nowhere is this more true than in the kitchen. If you're the one responsible for the family's meals, you'd be amazed to discover how much time you spend planning them, shopping for them, and cooking them. A significant portion of your day is invested in making sure your family is well-fed. Here are some tips to add extra moments to your allotment of "time-for-me."

 Plan your meals for the week, then stick to your plan. If something sounds good on the spur of the moment, right it down for next week's menu. Writing down and then following through on your plan cuts the time you have to spend thinking about what to fix for dinner, which frees up more time for you.

 In the evening, when you're organizing for tomorrow, take a quick look at the menu to see whether you need to defrost, chop, or pick something up from the store on your way home tomorrow.

 Leftovers aren't leftovers if you made too much on purpose. Having chicken on Sunday? Make more than you need and shred the rest for chicken and noodles one night. In the mood for turkey? Buy a pound or two more than you need, and use it for a soup-and-sandwiches night or hot turkey manhattans.

 Who says you have to eat breakfast in the morning? Pancakes, eggs and bacon, and French toast are fast and easy dinners (and you won't hear the kids complain).

 Save your menus and use them again. Instead of spending a lot of time planning meals and then shopping for them, put yourself on a rotating schedule—say a six-week cycle—and you can lighten your planning load.

 Especially if you feel like you spend all your "free time" in the kitchen, make sure it's a pleasant experience. Put on music you particularly like, burn a candle if that's your style, put on your slippers (and maybe your robe, too) and relax as much as possible while you're finishing out the day. Cooking dinner in high heels and fixing supper in slippers are two completely different experiences, I assure you.

 Give yourself a break. Regularly. One night a week, if possible, skip cooking. Eat out or eat in and let someone else fix it. If 7-year-old Patsy just loves to make things with peanut butter, she's sure to invent a masterpiece if you let her. (Be forewarned, though: If she makes it, you'll have to eat it.)

 Have the basics on hand. Think about the things your family just can't do without—staples like macaroni and cheese, chicken breasts, turkey hot dogs, bread, milk, peanut butter, and chocolate-chip cookie dough ice cream (not all at the same meal, of course)—and make sure you've got them on hand. I try to have several different kinds of meats, vegetables, fruits, breads, cereals—you know the routine. Then maybe I can create a menu for the week based on the stuff I've already got and—voilá!—another free hour I don't have to spend at the grocery store.

 Some cooks like help, and some cooks don't. If you're in the kitchen, it's your domain; ask for what you want. If you'd like 30 minutes of quiet while you prepare supper, you're entitled to that. Explain it to the kids, or your spouse, or whoever, and cook in peace. You'll feel rested and more settled when you put dinner on the table.

Make-Ahead Meals

It's amazing what you can do when you start applying "the big picture" to meal planning. That's what they did in the old days, you know, when Pa brought home a deer and Ma and the young'uns ate venison 120 different times until spring brought a fresh crop of rabbits and squirrels.

In this day of fast everything, the idea of buying in bulk may seem foreign. And your budget might limit how much you buy and how often you buy it. But purchasing foods your family really likes, foods you know they'll eat, and having them on hand can save you quite a bit of time in both meal planning and shopping.

With a little thought, you can come up with a pretty hefty list of meals your family really likes. And with a little more thought, you can think of ways to cut down on the time it takes to prepare those meals so there's more time and energy left for you.

Here's an example. At our house, I can always be sure my kids will eat these meals:

 Home-made pizza.

 Spaghetti.

 Chicken, potatoes, and carrots cooked in gravy. (We call it "The Farm Supper.")

 Beef Stroganoff.

 Tuna casserole with peas. (Don't ask me—I have strange kids.)

 Ham, new potatoes, and green beans cooked all day in the slow cooker. (We call it "The Other Farm Supper.")

 Meatballs, mashed potatoes, and gravy.

That's just a sampling of the meals they like. One thing I have discovered as a working mother is that there's a quick way and a slow way to do everything. Each of those meals I just listed has a long form and a short form.

No doubt you've discovered this. Take spaghetti. You can make your own pasta. You can blanche the tomatoes and mush them, and add chopped onion and fresh oregano and basil and parsley, and you can stand over that pot for an hour, stirring faithfully to make a wonderful, aromatic, delightfully spicy spaghetti sauce. Or you can open a jar of store-bought sauce.

You got up at 6:00 A.M., got the kids to day care and school, worked all day, picked up the kids, and are standing there in front of the stove. Which are you going to choose?

Exactly. Me too.

Things like beef Stroganoff have become turkey Stroganoff at our house, with browned ground turkey, mushroom soup, low-fat sour cream (I'm trying to be conscientious), and salt and pepper. Put this over cooked noodles and serve with a vegetable—dinner in 20 minutes, most of it simmering while I change clothes or look through Christopher's school papers.

Favorite Meals . . . Faster

What are the meals your family likes, and how can you fix them easier and faster?

Favorite Meals   Faster Version

_____   _____

_____   _____

_____   _____

_____   _____

Make-Ahead Meatballs

Hey, admit it—everybody loves meatballs. If you're not a beef eater, ground turkey can be rolled into meatballs, too. But who wants to stand over a skillet for 45 minutes, turning all those little balls each time one side is brown? (How many sides do those things *have*, anyway?)

Make a bunch of meatballs quickly by mixing up your favorite meatball recipe and pressing the mixture into one large rectangle on a cookie sheet. Cut the mixture in a cross-cross pattern, making a few dozen meatballs. Yes, they're square, but you can bake them at 350 degrees for 35 minutes, cool them, and pack them in freezer bags to keep for two months. Then throw them into soups, subs, spaghetti, Stroganoff, whatever you've got that needs a meatball on top.

To take part of the rush out of the dinnertime crazies, make up a "kit" with everything you need to set the table—dishes, silverware, napkins, whatever you use. Put it all in a big basket on the table. When it's time to set the table, your "helpers" have everything they need at the table, so they won't be under your feet. After dinner, make sure whoever does the dishes repacks the kit, putting the dishes, silverware, and napkins back in the basket for tomorrow night's dinner. You'll be amazed how much time this can save, and you'll never again have to run back to the kitchen, saying "We forgot the forks!"

And If You Love to Cook ...

There's a time and place for creative cooking too, especially if it's something you really enjoy. If you like to cook new and exciting recipes, and make a great mess doing it, give yourself time to have that pleasure. But consider where and when—and if you'll have the energy to clean up the mess once you've made it. On a work night, something fast, simple, and clean is a lot more appealing. Save your gourmet experiences for weekends and holidays.

Have These On-Hand for Quick Fixes

Bags of premixed salad
Salad dressing
Breads, buns, bagels
Pizza shells or refrigerated dough
Frozen vegetables
Pasta-vegetable mixes
Chicken patties, microwavable
Frozen fish fillets
Hot dogs, sliced meats, peanut butter
Cheese, sliced and grated
Sauces and sauce mixes
Eggs
Milk
Fruits
Yogurt

Cheater's Lasagna

Nine lasagna noodles, cooked

One jar spaghetti sauce

One large container small curd cottage cheese

Mozzarella slices

Parmesan cheese

Grease a 13"-by-9" baking dish; lay three noodles on the bottom. Top with half of the sauce; top with half of the cottage cheese. Top that with mozzarella slices and 2 tablespoons parmesan cheese. Repeat. Bake for 30 minutes in a 350-degree oven; then let it sit for 10 minutes before cutting. (If you have the time and the inclination, you can add browned sausage, hamburger, or turkey to the sauce.)

Even faster: Prepare the lasagna on the weekend, when you have time, and freeze it until you need it.

Even better: Next time you make lasagna, make two and freeze one.

Where Does the Time Go?

One of the easiest ways to find more time for yourself is to look at how you spend your time now. Do you spend a lot of time and energy on things that aren't important to you? Do you insist on doing things yourself that you could delegate? Put a notebook in your pocket for a few days and keep track of what time you spend doing what. How long is your commute? How long did you spend explaining a policy to a coworker that she could have looked up in the manual? Why were you the one picking up 1,200 plastic building blocks from the living room carpet? (You weren't the one playing with them, were you?)

Where Does the Time Go?

7:00 _____

7:30 _____

8:00 _____

*** Work time ***

12:00 _____

12:30 _____

*** Work time ***

5:00 _____

5:30 _____

6:00 _____

6:30 _____

7:00 _____

7:30 _____

8:00 _____

8:30 _____

9:00 _____

9:30 _____

10:00 _____

From One Parent to Another
"I believe it's important to give extra love touches to the children in our time together at home."
—Mother of three who works part-time

Making the Moment Count

Once you've logged your time for a few days, take a look at your notes. What stands out? Where could you pick up more time? We all have a certain number of things to do in a day, but you might be able to reorder (or weed out) your To-Do list to get yourself some R&R time. Here are a few suggestions:

Do you drive to work? If you drive, make notes to yourself (get one of those hand-held tape recorders) about things you need to take care of later. Or dictate a letter to someone you need to catch up with. Or work on the report you were planning to do tonight after the kids are in bed. Then, tonight, you can watch a movie, relax in a hot bath, play pool with your spouse, or just cuddle on the couch instead of working.

Do you ride to work? If you commute, you have a block of time when you may be just staring out the window or engaging in idle conversation. While staring out the window and idle conversation are both worthwhile activities in moderation, spending each day in this mode keeps you from having more R&R time for yourself. On the commute, you can catch up with paperwork, balance your checkbook, make your grocery list, write a letter, plan an upcoming birthday party, or do any number of things that might otherwise take up evening time.

What do you do for lunch? Hopefully, eat. But beyond that, you could be using your lunch hour to get yourself more free time later in the day. Designate one or two days a week as "errand" days, when you do things like pick up the cleaning, shop for the holidays, get the car's oil changed, go to the bank, whatever. On the other three days, of course, go to lunch with friends, coworkers, or your spouse. The social interaction is just as important as the let-down time later. But using one or two lunches a week to get ahead on the "have-tos" in your life can make a big difference in how much time you have left over for yourself.

Do you know when you've done enough?
When I first began keeping a To-Do list, I didn't have the right idea. I'd ask myself each morning, "What do I have to get done today?" I'd make a list of 10 or 12 things I had to get done. Throughout my workday, I'd go at the items, one by one, crossing them off as I finished them.

Fine. I was doing fine.

But then I'd start thinking of other things. "Oh yeah," I'd remember, "I promised to get Kelly's skates sharpened. And those books are due next Tuesday; I could take them back today. And I suppose I could start on chapter 3 and get a jump on my deadline . . . "

Wrong. My To-Do list grew all day long. By the end of the day, I had more things left to do than I had when I started. The list might be 30 or 40 items long. How do you think I felt at the end of the day? The phrase "swimming in quicksand" comes to mind.

If you're going to keep a To-Do list, write down the things you need to get done (be realistic), and when you've crossed them all off, stop. Celebrate. Take that bubble bath. Watch the football game. You decided what you wanted to accomplish today, and you accomplished it. Now it's time to rest.

One of the best gifts you can give another person is the gift of your full attention. As you make an effort to consolidate tasks and get more done with less work, remember to listen carefully and respond to those who need you to be present right now—little kids and big kids alike.

The Art of Simplicity

There's a lot to be said for simplicity. The older we get, the more responsibilities we add, the more complicated our lives seem to get. Especially when you work and you're a parent, there are a lot of things to do, and everything seems important. It takes a fair amount of thought—invested up front—to reduce the number of details in your life so the important things can stand out.

Sometimes we add responsibilities we don't really need. We say, "Okay," when they call us to run the cookie sale. We can't say no to subbing for the first baseman at Thursday night softball. The PTO needs help—and if we don't do it, who will? Randy has to be at play practice three times a week for the next month, and guess who gets to drive him? Life sometimes seems like an endless series of details demanding our attention. As John Lennon put it, "Life is what happens to you while you're making other plans."

Once you've examined where you're spending your time, it might be easy to see where you can eliminate things that aren't worth either the priority or the effort. The suggestions in this section will help get you started thinking about applying the Art of Simplicity to your own life.

Simplify Priorities

When you ask yourself what your personal priorities are, do you come up with a list of 10 or 12 items? A priority is what's most important. If you're carrying around 10 "most important" issues in your life, you may want to think about what's truly *most* important and trim your list accordingly.

Remember in chapter 1, when you and your family came up with a list of family priorities? Those should fit here, as well. When you're looking at your life and your choices with a "time-for-me" perspective, expect your own personal priorities to be slightly different from—but still in line with—your family priorities. There will be times when the priorities of the family come before your personal priorities (for example, you need to fix the furnace when you'd really rather be soaking in a hot tub). And there will be times when your personal priorities come before the family priorities (everyone has a right to be heard, but you really need 10 minutes of quiet).

If you aren't used to thinking about yourself and what's important to you, this may be a difficult task. Sit down with a piece of paper and write your answer to the question, "What's most important to me?" Whether you come up with two or twenty answers, write them all down. Once you see what's in your head, written down in black and white, you can begin the process of weeding out the unimportant things. As you look through your list, one or two items will emerge that are truly important. The rest are just situations to deal with, not issues you must treat with supreme importance. Simply knowing that something is not a matter of "life or death" can make stress evaporate like a puddle on a summer sidewalk.

Just get them down on paper. That's a start.

What's Most Important to Me?

_____

_____

_____

_____

Simplify Time Investments

Some things you simply don't have to do. Do *you* have to be the one to take Jesse to hockey every other day? Can you arrange to trade off with another parent or with your spouse? Do you *really* need to make four trips to the grocery every week or, with a little time management and planning, could you consolidate them into one trip? Do you spend more time on the phone than you want to? Would organizing a phone time when you return calls to friends and relatives save some time for you in the long run?

When you examine your priorities and recognize the two or three things you really want to spend your time on, you're free to decide how much time to spend on those things. The time you spend on unimportant things becomes less and less. You begin looking for people to delegate those tasks to. You begin spending more time on the things that really matter to you, the things you need to see through to completion yourself.

What Could I Spend Less Time On?

_____

_____

_____

_____

Simplify Material Possessions

In many ways, we don't really own our possessions—they own us. The more things we have, the more we have to take care of: dusting and polishing, washing and waxing, servicing, repairing, insuring, improving. Don't wait for a garage sale; go through your possessions and ask yourself what you use and what you don't, what you want and what you're ready to let go. Think of your things in terms of how much time, trouble, and money they cost you. Then compare the cost with the pleasure they bring you, the convenience they offer, and so on. The bottom line? If you want it, keep it; but remember, the investment you make in your possessions is more than a monetary one.

Start by making a list of the possessions that take up a lot of your time. If you're spending two hours every Saturday morning fixing the lawn mower, for example, maybe it's time to get a new lawn mower. Once you determine which of your possessions, if any, are possessing you, you can decide what to do about it.

What Things Do I Spend Time On?

_____

_____

_____

_____

_____

_____

Simplify Commitments

Sometimes it's other people—and our reaction to their expectations—that keep us busy with things that aren't priorities. Do you say "Yes" to everything? If you're not sure, watch yourself through the course of a day and see how many times you volunteer for something no one else wants to do, suggest a solution that involves work on your part, or say "Yes" when inside you wish you could say "No." When they ask you to be editor of the historical society's newsletter, you might be honored, but you might also be pressed for time. A clear, "No, thank you," frees you of the responsibility and lets the society look for someone who has the time and inclination for the job.

How can you evaluate which commitments are important and which ones you should pass by? Any commitment you accept should meet these criteria:

 It should fit your time constraints; you shouldn't have to rearrange your life to fulfill it.

 It should be worth what it costs you in effort, investment, and family time.

 It should be fun, challenging, or stretch your creative spirit.

You may not need to relinquish any of the commitments you have now; or you may, after careful thought, decide to keep a few and release those that are taking time you don't want to invest. With the return to work, you need to be more protective of your time, so think carefully about commitments you make in the future.

And, even if you trim back your commitments now, it doesn't mean you will always be "uninvolved." One mother put it this way:

◆ ◆

*"When I first went back to work, it was all I could do
to get the kids to school, work all day, get home,
cook dinner, clean a little, and fall into bed at night.
On the weekends, I caught up on all the housework I
didn't do during the week. I had to give up many
outside commitments, because it was all I could do
to live my life. After about six months, things got
easier, and I started being a room mother again.
Then, a few months later, I started teaching Sunday
school. Gradually, as my life balanced, I got back into
the swing of things."*

◆ ◆

The moral? Do only what you can do comfortably,
and remember that you and your family are all
learning how to balance home and work issues.

What Are My Commitments?

_____

_____

_____

_____

_____

Saying no isn't easy, especially when you're not
used to doing it. But sidestep the commitment
early if you get any of these warnings:

 You know you don't want to do it.

 You feel coerced or guilty.

 People are appealing to you with a "But no
one else can take care of this" approach. (If
no one else is willing to help, there must be a
reason why.)

The clearer you are about your priorities, the easier it is to say no to commitments you don't want. When someone asks you to head the neighborhood task force, check it against your priority list. If it doesn't fit—especially if it will take away from one of your top priorities—just say no.

Simplify Unimportant Jobs

BEST &
WORST

Worst:
"Missing out on the most valuable time in the children's lives, as they'll be grown before we know it"

The keyword here is *delegate.* Are you still taking out the trash every Tuesday night, even though you've got three teenagers in the house? Do you really have to be the one who washes the dishes morning and night? Do you spend time standing by the copy machine at work when your assistant has nothing to do? If you can release the jobs that don't have to be done by you personally, you free yourself up to get more done in the time you've got. That translates directly to more R&R time at home. Another benefit of delegating is that it gives the kids a chance to contribute to the family, to feel needed, instead of being "guests" in their own home.

Which Jobs Could I Delegate?

Job

To Whom?

_____   _____

_____   _____

_____   _____

_____   _____

_____   _____

Simplify Kids

Ha! If there were some magic formula to this, we'd all be millionaires. But it *is* possible to simplify life with kids if you stay focused on what's important. This, like everything else in parenting, has to be grounded in reality: You can't just sidestep making Tim clean his room because you'd rather do something pleasant. It's a continual process of refocusing on why you're doing what you're doing, and asking yourself whether that's how you need to spend your time and energy right now.

This is a hard issue for me, especially around the holidays. We want to schedule everything. Out for a holiday dinner this night. To a concert that night. Making Christmas cookies today, making candy tomorrow. Pick up the kids at this time, be at Mom's for dinner by that time.

In the hectic pace, people can—and often do—get cranky. Teenagers rebel. Toddlers have tantrums. The rest of us get headaches.

How can we simplify this mess? By focusing on what's important. Is spending time with the kids most important, or is cleaning the kitchen most important? (There is no right answer here; either could be most important in different circumstances.) If you remember to ask yourself the question, "What's most important here?" the answer becomes very clear, and you stop feeling like you've got to accomplish 20 things before bedtime.

See? It's simple. Almost.

Saving Time

I spend more time than I'd like on _____

_____

_____

_____

I could solve this by _____

_____

_____

_____

What Will You Do with Your Free Time?

Some people don't think about their free time because they don't have any. And if they did, they wouldn't know what to do with it. If you're one of those people, a little daydreaming is in order.

Perhaps we should define "free time." A month-long sabbatical is certainly free time, but that's probably not possible for most of us. Free time, in the context of most working parents, is an occasional spare hour at the end of the day, a few hours on the weekend, perhaps a long weekend getaway.

For best results, especially if you're not used to having any free time at all, start small. Logging how you spend your time (which you did earlier in this chapter) will show you where your time is going. The next logical step is thinking about where you *want* the time to go.

What You Need Is a Hobby!

Can't you just see it—a young mother with a baby on her hip, the chicken she'd meant to thaw for dinner in one hand, her briefcase open by her feet, the phone cocked on her shoulder, reading from a report while she paces around the kitchen. Tell this woman she needs a hobby, and you'd better duck; frozen poultry hurts!

Unless you had a hobby before your kids were born, it's unlikely you'll have the time or energy to acquire a new hobby while they are small. A hobby is simply something you're interested in, something you do for fun, something that isn't you (1) earning a living, (2) being a parent, (3) being an employee, or (4) being a spouse. A hobby is something you like to do just because you like to do it.

The word "hobby" tends to put a trivial-sounding front on the concept, but it's something you should consider. When you're not being Mom or Dad, Wife or Husband, Daughter or Son, Employee or Employer, what do you like to do? There might be a clue there that could lead you to an enjoyable way to spend your free time.

 You might try a hobby that your kids can do with you, like making model cars or planes, arts and crafts, or gourmet cooking. Remember, however, that it should be relaxing and fun—not something that adds to your stress.

What a hobby isn't:

 Something you do with your spouse so you can have more "together" time. (That's your spouse's hobby, not yours.)

 Something you do because it's "good" for you. (If you don't really want to do it, don't do it.)

 Something you "should" do. ("I *should* learn French so I can converse better with our foreign affiliates.")

What Do I Like to Do?

_____

_____

_____

_____

Expand Your Horizons

When you're thinking about what you'd like to do in your downtime, consider taking a class or learning more about something that has always interested you. There doesn't need to be any practical application; just learn it because you want to.

How can you expand your horizons? Here are a few ideas:

 Take a cooking class.

 See a movie that's different from the kind you usually see.

 Go online and chat with computer users across town or across the world.

 Read about an upcoming holiday and learn how other cultures celebrate it.

 Try camping.

 Look through _The New Yorker_ and _MAD Magazine_ in the same afternoon.

 Watch cartoons with your kids.

 Audition for a part in a community theater production.

Listen to music outside your usual tastes.

 Spend a rainy afternoon at the library.

Horizon Expanders

What would I like to try in my free time?

_____

_____

_____

There's really only one answer to the question, "What should you do with your free time?" The answer is, "Anything you want to." Contrary to popular opinion, free time is not free at all. It comes at a cost. The time and effort you invest in work and family earn you whatever time you can find for yourself. And, chances are, it's less time than you deserve.

The next section lists some ways you can improve yourself and your lifestyle by using your time in healthy ways.

Tips for Self-Rewards

What kinds of things can you do to reward yourself in your free moments? Think about things you really like—activities, foods, experiences, places—and make a list of ways you can pay yourself back for trying so hard and doing such a good job. Make a list of big things and little things.

Little rewards are for things like not blowing up at the dinner table, or getting everybody to school and work on time. A little reward could be a night out, a bubble bath, a new CD, a chocolate eclair, or a night on the couch in your bathrobe.

Save big rewards for longer-term accomplishments: paying off a particular bill, finishing a project, meeting a deadline, making it through your first month of work, handling an important meeting, or resolving a difficult circumstance. A big reward could be an outfit or piece of equipment you've been wanting (even if you put it on layaway), a day in the country, an evening out, a trip to the theater, or something else you've been longing for.

Take Good Care of Yourself

We've talked about the practical issues involved in finding time for yourself and discussed some of the ways people use their free time. The fitness craze is one of America's latest full-blown explosions—and for good reason. Most of us recognize that, in order to get healthy and stay there, we need to take better care of our bodies—and that means what we eat and what kinds of exercise we get. We've seen the statistical and physical link between exercise and health. Researchers have shown that we feel less stress, live longer, and cope better if we exercise on a regular basis. Okay, we're sold. Now it's just a matter of finding the time—and the routine—and sticking with it.

Work Out? When?

Who has time to go to a gym? Not many of us. Unless your company has an on-site workout room or there's a local gym that really is "local" to your home or office, setting a time to work out— and then doing it regularly—is a hard commitment to make.

If you like the contact with other adults and want to participate in a class, most communities offer courses in tennis, racquetball, golf, yoga, or aerobics. Some gyms even offer baby-sitting or classes for the kids, and the extra, outside work contact is a good thing.

But many of us are getting the workout equipment ourselves and setting up our own home gyms. Last year, Americans spent more than $2.5 billion on home exercise equipment. The most popular pieces of equipment were (in this order) stair climbers, aerobic steps, stationary bikes, ski machines, and treadmills.

There are workouts for every body type, energy level, and age group. "Workout" doesn't necessarily mean weight-lifting or track-running. Yoga and tai chi are both popular modes of exercise that enable you to work out gently, strengthening and toning your muscles, without the athletic-style training so popular today.

The Basic Workout—Parent Style

Whether you use special equipment or simply do bends, stretches, and toe-touches on your own, moving is the important thing. And it takes less of an investment than you might think.

Experts say that exercising 20 minutes (less time than you spend watching one news show) five times a week will make a difference, especially if your routine is focused and intense.

What kind of exercise should you do? Before you start any new kind of physical regimen, consult your doctor. He or she may have some suggestions about the types of exercise that will best serve your physical needs.

As you think about putting together an exercise program, consider these basic guidelines:

 Start and end with stretching. Every exercise routine needs a warm-up and a cool-down. Slow stretches for your back, legs, and arms prepare your muscles for the coming increase in activity and raise your heart rate gradually. On the other side of your workout, stretching helps your heart rate to return gradually to normal.

When stretching, experts agree that maintaining the longest stretch you can for a moment or two is more helpful and better for you than "bobbing" to a stretch that's hard for you and immediately releasing it. It's not how far you get, it's how well you get there, that counts.

The Home Stretch

One great wake-up stretch is a yoga position that stretches and lengthens the spine. You'll feel lighter and clearer as you stretch all the sleep out of your system:

1. Sit on the floor, in a kneeling position. (If this hurts either your ankles or your knees, put a rolled-up towel across your ankles before you sit back on them.)

2. Lean forward until your forehead touches the floor.

3. Stretch first your right arm, then your left, straight over your head and place your palms down on the floor.

4. Walk your fingers up as far as you can reach. Hold to a count of 10. Remember to breathe slowly and evenly as you stretch.

5. Push up from your kneeling position to straighten your legs. You should now be in a triangle position, with your hands and feet evenly spaced and flat on the floor.

6. Push your hip bones up toward the ceiling and hold to a count of 5. This stretches your spine and releases all the little knots and tight places that accumulated while you slept.

7. Slowly return to the kneeling position; then walk yourself up to sitting using your hands as supports.

8. Take several deep breaths and exhale slowly before standing.

 Do what you like. When you're planning your workout, be sure to include activities you like. If running isn't your thing, try something else. Popular and beneficial exercises you can do at home include knee bends, toe touches, side bends, leg lifts, and jumping jacks.

 Listen to your body. We're all different, and our bodies react to activities differently. Be sure to get advice from your doctor on things you need to consider when designing an exercise program. Aches and pains are not unusual, especially at first, when your body is not used to the exercise. But if you are having chronic pain or feel something sharp and stabbing, like a pulled muscle or some other kind of injury, back off your program until you get professional advice.

Pain in the Back?

A great exercise for relieving simple back pain—caused by standing for too long, lifting something you shouldn't, or carrying too much stress without a break—takes just a minute and enough room to lay down:

1. Lay down on your back on a bed, couch, or the floor.

2. Take a deep breath and exhale slowly.

3. As you exhale, push the small of your back toward the floor.

4. Inhale and allow your back to return to normal.

5. Exhale and press your back to the floor once again.

A simple variation: If your back is feeling tight in addition to being sore, put one hand on the floor at the small of your back; then when you exhale, press your back against your hand. This modified intensity still releases some tension, and the counter-pressure of your hand helps the muscles relax.

According to Peter Bernstein and Christopher Ma, authors of *The Practical Guide to Practically Everything*, the best exercises for stress reduction are bicycling, cross-country skiing, jogging, running, rowing, canoeing, and walking.[1]

Generally, however, the experts say you should just move. Don't worry too much about the type of aerobic exercise you do. Do it all. Try anything. Just move. They all burn calories, and varying your workout will reduce boredom, which means you will stick with it longer.

An Afternoon Wake-Me-Up

Do you get the 2:00 drag? If you're feeling fuzzy mid-afternoon and need to get the blood circulating back to your brain, you can try this one right at your desk:

1. Take a deep breath; exhale slowly.

2. Nod your head forward as far as you can; repeat three times.

3. Lean your head back as far as you can; repeat three times.

4. Nod your head toward your left shoulder; repeat three times.

5. Nod your head toward your right shoulder; repeat three times.

6. Allow your head to roll forward and then rotate around left, back, right, and straighten.

7. Repeat entire exercise two more times.

Your neck will feel more relaxed, and you'll feel more awake and invigorated.

A few suggestions:

 Stop if anything hurts.

 Especially at first, don't push too hard. Stop as soon as you feel tired or if you become short of breath.

 Do warm-up and cool-down stretching before and after your exercise session.

 Concentrate on doing the exercise right rather than quickly. Form is more important than speed. When you're stretching, stretch full out and hold the stretch. It's much better for you than stretching-releasing, stretching-releasing a number of times.

Increase weight, resistance, and pressure gradually. Build up a little at a time, over many days (or even weeks). Improving your physical condition is a process, not something you can achieve in a few afternoons.

 Be realistic. If you follow a simple exercise plan, you'll see some changes—tightening, toning, strengthening—in 6 to 12 weeks.

 Some families do their exercise together. Try a 30-minute walk after dinner. Or tennis early in the morning, before it gets hot. Or, for the really zealous, a 20-minute wake-up workout is sure to get your family's day off to a rousing start.

Been There, Done That

As a working parent, it's likely you are already exercising more than you realize. Those trips up and down the stairs carrying laundry? That's exercise. Walking to the mailbox? Exercise. Mowing the grass, sweeping, bringing in the trash cans, trimming the bushes? Those all qualify. The trick is to be conscious of what you're doing, use your muscles, and breath. If you've got to be doing it anyway, you might as well get the full physical benefit of the experience.

Exercise, Exercise

This is what I already do for exercise: _____

_____

_____

_____

_____

I'd be willing to try this: _____

_____

_____

_____

_____

The Power of Touch

Have you ever been stressed to the limit when one of your kids, or your spouse, walked up and gave you a hug? It's an amazing phenomenon—your chest lightens, the clenching releases. You probably sighed a great sigh, and allowed yourself to be embraced.

The power of touch is something medical science is exploring more and more, and we have only to see our effects on others—and their effects on us—to know that there's something healing about touching and being touched by someone you care about.

As part of your stress-reducing and self-rewarding plans, consider these ideas:

   Hug your kids more.

   Ask for hugs.

Touch people you care about when you talk to them.

 Hold hands with your spouse.

 Rub your neck when you begin feeling stressed. (Or ask your spouse to do it for you.)

 Cuddle up with your kids when you read to them.

 Learn to give and receive back rubs.

 Read a book on foot reflexology and experiment on yourself or your family.

 When your kids are grumpy or unruly, touch them gently. I learned this with my son when he was 2. When he was on the verge of a tantrum, if I smoothed his hair off his forehead, he would invariably calm down enough that we could avoid a tirade.

Summary

In this chapter, you've thought a little about what you can do for yourself as you adjust to all the life changes going on around you. Finding time for yourself is an important part of staying happy and healthy. If you observe where you are spending your time now, you might be able to find places where you can pick up more free time. You can then decide where you want to invest that free time—whether it's with family and friends, or just for yourself.

Notes

1. Peter Bernstein and Christopher Ma, *The Practical Guide to Practically Everything* (New York: Random House, 1995).

Chapter
9

Creating a Family-Friendly Workplace

"Happiness is having a large, loving, caring, close-knit family in another city."
—George Burns

Family values are getting a great deal of attention in the '90s. In homes all across the country, parents are striving to make the best possible decisions for their children's futures. We seem to have reached an agreement of some kind: Family values are a critical ingredient to raising happy, healthy children. And parents aren't the only ones raising the family values banner. Teachers are teaching them, preachers are preaching them, and politicians are promising them. And businesses are beginning to understand that creating a family-friendly environment works in the best interest of their employees and in their own best interest, as well: A happy employee is a productive employee.

What Is a Family-Friendly Workplace?

Family-friendly employers come in different shapes and sizes. When you were job hunting, hopefully you found a place that embraces the issues that come with child-raising and that is fairly liberal about things like phone calls from home, flexible scheduling, and pinch-hitting in unexpected circumstances. Not all employers are able to offer such services as on-site day care, child-care subsidies, or schedules that allow you to divide time between home and work. If your company cannot offer these, that does not mean it is not family-friendly or in line with family values.

Family-friendly is an attitude, not a perk. It's not the number of days you can take off for personal time, it's the attitude the company takes toward the needed leave of absence. A company that embraces the family is a family-friendly company. If your company—no matter how small or large it is—understands the importance of the family core and encourages its employees to value their families, you are in a supportive, family-friendly environment.

What You Can Do:
Start a newsletter that includes a parents' Q&A column.

Can One Person Make a Family-Friendly Workplace?

Sue was a great boss. She was pleasant, direct, and challenging, and understood what it was like to raise a family and hold down a full-time career. She had no problem with your getting an afternoon call from the kids or taking a long lunch so you could get Andrew to the dentist, as long as you made up the time or the work during the week. And when Elizabeth had the flu last winter, Sue suggested you take your computer home for a few days and work there. But not long ago, Sue got promoted, and now a new boss has been brought into your department. She's not pleased with the phone calls. And when you asked to take off early Friday afternoon so you could go to Andrew's teacher's conference, she said, "I hope you're not going to make a habit of this."

While it's not unusual to work directly for someone who understands family priorities, one person does not make a family-friendly workplace. Having a boss with a similar understanding of family issues makes life easier, to be sure, but the true mark of a family-friendly workplace is in its personnel policies and can be felt in the hallways. You know when your family is welcome at work—even if only in spirit—and when you're supposed to leave the Mom or Dad part of your heart at home.

Family Realities for Employers—and How You Can Benefit

Whether you are working for a 2-person business or a 2,000-employee corporation, the current steps toward family-friendliness in the workplace are sure to help you balance home and office more easily. Throughout this book, we've focused on the great things you bring to the workplace because of your family core. Your family responsibilities—and the values they represent to you—can make you a strong, capable, insightful, and dedicated employee.

Having children—or, more specifically, having and honoring family responsibilities—is not a liability, nor should it be considered one. Today's parents are trying hard to balance home and work, providing the best quality care for their families and the highest possible service to their employers. A person who can pull that off must be intelligent, capable, responsible, creative, and determined.

Employers want employees who bring those kinds of qualities to the job. They have less turnover; lower retraining costs; and dedicated, hard-working staffs.

What You Can Do:
Organize a pitch-in picnic for your department and make sure spouses and kids are invited.

But the nature of the workforce is changing. More and more, employers are having to adapt to the worker who is discovering life—perhaps for the first time—outside the walls of the office. That worker could be a young mother who wants to work at home after the birth of a child; a father who wants Thursday afternoons off to coach Little League; a long-distance commuter who wants to work a two-day-in, three-day-out schedule; or a single employee who wants to work and go to grad school at the same time.

Slow Change Is Better Than No Change

Your employer may be going through growing pains as the company evaluates different ways to find and keep good employees and provide them with the flexibility and programs they need to take good care of their families. Watch for these signs that your company is changing:

 More employees with family responsibilities are being hired.

Better benefit packages are offered.

 A suggestion box goes up in human resources.

 A new company newsletter appears and invites employee participation.

 Leadership and interpersonal communication workshops are held.

 There are new, corporate-sponsored health policies.

Whether you see signs of change or you're still waiting for a glimmer of hope, remember that seeds need time to grow. Companies—especially large ones—can be slow to change and will be sure to investigate every possible angle before implementing new policies that will change peoples' lives and the way they do business. Be patient and supportive of your employer while these changes are being explored (and, hopefully, added), and keep the lines of communication as open as possible so that your opinion is welcomed and valued.

Employers are trying to figure out how to bend enough to allow their employees to grow and be happy while still getting the quality, dedication, and productivity they need to maintain a successful business. It's a tall order, and one that may make your employer more receptive to your ideas on how to balance the work/family issue from both perspectives. How can this "open-mindedness" benefit you as a working parent?

Businesses are less willing to rely on tradition. "We've never done it that way before" is not a reason to avoid trying it now. More and more, employers are listening to what employees need and want and implementing programs and benefits to address the changing needs of the workforce. Just because your company has never had Family Day before doesn't mean the time isn't ripe now.

Businesses are recognizing that the most successful companies are creative problem-solvers. If you're having trouble with a particular policy or attitude, spend some time thinking about what the problem is and why you're having it. You may be able to come up with a creative response to the situation that no one has thought of yet. If you can propose a "win-win" solution, you may have a shot at solving your own problem and making things better for other employees, as well.

 More businesses are looking into cross-training employees. Especially in large corporations where job-sharing is common, cross-training employees (training employees to do multiple tasks) cuts down on the overall costs of training and allows employers to be more flexible when an employee needs time off for family or personal reasons. If you have a chance to improve your skills or learn new ones on the job, take the opportunity. This might lead to increased flexibility for you and make you a more valuable employee, as well.

Businesses Need to Communicate Policies Clearly

When employers add a new program or benefit, they do well to publish a "how to get involved" sheet and circulate information on what they expect of employees in return (how many days' notice before a leave of absence, sign-up times for day-care programs, how to arrange swing shifts or job-sharing situations, etc.). If your company does not have a document like this, suggest one. Getting policies in black and white will help your employer consider current policies and perhaps begin a discussion for family-friendly additions.

What You Can Do:
*Put up a flier advertising your
son's Boy Scout paper drive and
enlist the support of your work group.*

**More businesses are making employee
health their concern.** Employers offer
health plans to full-time employees; that's
nothing new. But today more employers are
offering wellness plans—plans that focus on
helping employees stay healthy, manage
stress, balance responsibilities, feel better
about themselves, and work through
emotional issues. This wellness approach is a
great service to the employee, but it is good
for the employer as well. With a small
investment of money and time, the
employer can ensure that employees are
happier, healthier, and more well-adjusted,
which translates to a stronger staff for the
company. If your company is considering
this kind of program, you might want to
suggest including family activities—Saturday
morning jogs in the park, a lunchtime yoga
class—or sponsoring family agencies through
participation in walk-a-thons, runs-for-fun, or
other community-action projects.

BEST &
WORST

*Best:
"Having
a family to
work for
and come
home to."*

Employers are realizing that the focus of the
workforce is changing. Their real challenge
is not to find the employee who will sign on
body and soul and then burn out early, but
rather to keep their well-rounded, mature
employees focused, energized, and inspired.
They are recognizing what all working
parents know: It's the long-term relationship
that blossoms over time. It's simply a matter
of envisioning, implementing, and
evaluating ways employers, employees, and
their families can grow and succeed
together.

Helping Your Company Start an On-Site Day Care

Running an on-site day-care facility isn't feasible for many businesses. An employer needs available floor space and—after checking with state requirements—will undoubtedly have to remodel to create a facility that meets with government codes.

If you're thinking of proposing to your employer that he or she start an on-site facility, you'd better do your homework first by answering these questions:

 Is there enough room?

 Is there enough interest? (How many working parents are there in your company? How many of them will use the day care?)

 Are the children involved young enough that creating a facility makes sense? (If most of the children are 8 or older, for example, they won't be needing child care much longer. If your company is continually hiring young families with infants and toddlers, however, the need for continual child care is greater.)

 What building codes and state requirements will you need to look into?

 Approximately how long would it take to get the center open?

 Approximately how much of an investment would be required? (There will be costs of construction and renovation, as well as monthly staffing costs, footage costs, and other overhead expenditures.)

Getting answers to these questions
may take quite a bit of phone tag, so
don't go scouting until you're fairly
sure your employer will be receptive
to the idea or, at least, that you have
enough of a parental following to
sway the interest of the boss.

What does your employer need in order to get
started? Once you've got the answers to the basic
questions, call your state health and human
services department to find out about
requirements for on-site day cares. You'll be able
to get information on building codes, health issues,
teacher-to-child ratios, meal planning, and other
items regulated in professional care of children.

To find out more about different
types of programs and funding
options for day care, check out
Laurie Blum's *Free Money for Day
Care.*[1]

What You Can Do:
*Give a talk at your child's school
career day about what you do
and the service your company offers.
(Good for the business, great for the kids!)*

Helping Your Company Start a Subsidy Program

Many companies now subsidize the cost of child
care for their employees. KinderCare, one of the
largest for-profit child-care providers in the

country, offers a corporate sponsoring program called Kindustry. In the program, KinderCare offers a 10 percent discount to employers, who then pay between 20 and 30 percent of the total day-care cost for employees. As an employee of a company that participates in such a program, you may pay only 60 percent of your total child-care costs, which could reduce your bill by $40 or more a week.

If you plan to approach your company about a subsidy program, have the answers to these questions ready:

 How many employees in your company have small children?

 What kinds of problems will a day-care subsidy solve?

 What are the day-care centers in your area? (You might want to call and see if any have subsidy programs already.)

 What costs can the employer expect? Can you show how this will benefit the employer in the long run?

 Who should the employer contact to discuss subsidy arrangements?

Day-Care Information Sheet

Local Day-Care Centers   Contact

_____   _____

_____   _____

_____   _____

_____   _____

_____   _____

Alternative Care Options

Even if your company doesn't offer one of these larger family-friendly options, it may have other programs in place, or the boss may be willing to entertain the idea. Here are a couple of options to look into.

Flexible Work Times

There are several different programs like this throughout the country. Call it flex-time, job-sharing, whatever—you might be able to get the time off you need if you only ask. Some companies, such as IBM, offer employees two-hour flex-time periods in the middle of the day so they can take care of child-care issues, volunteer at school, whatever. Sue leaves her job as a systems administrator on Tuesday afternoons to teach her daughter Kami's computer class at the local elementary school. It's fun for Sue and good for Kami, and fosters good will for Sue's employer. Everybody wins.

Flexible Leave Policies

Congress passed the Family Medical Leave Act (FMLA) in 1993 to ensure short-term guaranteed leave to people who need or want to take care of dependents. FMLA can be used after the birth or adoption of a child or for emergency medical care, and is mandated for companies with more than 50 employees. Your company may have other leave policies in place, including sick day, personal day, and vacation day policies. Be sure to ask about these and other policies, such as extended leave (with or without pay), the option to work at home while caring for a sick child, or half-time or swing-time options that enable you to work fewer hours for a specified period of time.

What You Can Do:
*Take your daughter to work
on National Take-Your-Daughter-To-Work Day.*

From One Parent to Another
*"Take your kids to work with you
whenever you can. I work with a
social service agency, so my kids get to
do things like deliver presents to needy
families over the holidays. It's good for them
to see how other people live. They realize
people are different and their homes, values, and
priorities all vary."*
—Mother of two who works part-time

Starting a Discussion with Your Employer

When you've got a suggestion you want your employer to consider, going the extra distance to make sure you've thought it through completely will help get it more than a cursory glance. Here are a few suggestions:

 Put it in writing. In as clear and attractive a form as you can, put your idea on paper. Make sure four things are addressed: (1) what problem will be solved if your idea is implemented; (2) how you plan to do it; (3) what involvement—financial or otherwise— is required of the employer; and (4) what the benefit will be.

 Have other parents review it. Suggestions from more than one or two people give the plan additional force. Having the interest of a number of parents means more to an employer than a single parent wanting a change.

Try to anticipate points of resistance and have alternatives ready. If you think the floor space is the weakest part of your plan, have two or three back-up suggestions to keep the boss thinking.

 At your first meeting, be happy to get an, "I'll think about it." In the corporate world, few suggestions get a go-ahead the first time out. Present your information in such a way that you are merely opening the door, so the discussion can continue in the future.

Yeah, But How Will That Help Us?

If your employer doesn't see how adding family-friendly programs will help the company—whether it's a day-care subsidy or simply allowing a Parents' Q&A bulletin board—use these points to enlighten him or her:

A happy employee is more likely to be a productive employee.

A happy employee is likely to stay on the job.

A happy employee is less likely to be sick, to have problems with tardiness, or to have difficulties with superiors or coworkers.

A happy employee is one of your best advertisements.

Sponsoring family-friendly programs spreads good will among employees and in the community.

Supporting family-friendly programs makes a statement of social responsibility to other area businesses.

The children being helped in family-friendly programs constitute the next generation of workers. By caring for children today, businesses are investing in their own futures.

A Little Support Can Mean a Lot

Even in a small business, you can set up family-friendly supports. It could be a lunch, an after-work meeting, or a bulletin board, but providing something that enables families to find each other and share concerns and resources is an important asset. This section provides a few suggestions that might start a family feeling at your workplace.

Parents' Lunch Out

One of the first things you'll want to do when you organize a parent's group is have a gathering where working parents can meet one another. With your employer's okay, you can organize a pitch-in on-site or an off-site luncheon at a local restaurant. Give parents the opportunity to get acquainted, and the group may simply form itself.

Remember that your employer, while being sensitive to your needs, also must be sensitive to those of other employees who are not parents. Whatever program, group, or support you suggest, make sure you welcome the participation of everyone in your company; don't exclude others based on any perceived differences.

Creating a Parents' Q&A Board

Another idea your employer might go along with is a Parents' Q&A bulletin board, or a section of the existing employee board where parents can set up carpooling arrangements and post names of back-up baby-sitters, parenting tips, or interesting and helpful articles.

Things to Put on a Parents' Q&A Board

- Organizing tips
- Child-care articles
- Names of good baby-sitters
- Notices of special classes
- Carpooling questions
- Schedule changes
- Special products
- Notices of upcoming events

Organizing Co-Ops

Once you know who the other working parents in your company are, you might want to do something like make cooperative child-care arrangements. You can do this yourself, without an employer subsidy.

For example, suppose that you and four other parents in your organization are looking for new child-care arrangements. You hear about a day-care home only two blocks from your office. You talk with the other parents and then approach the day-care provider to arrange for small-group care. You may be able to get a discount, as well as share pick-up and drop-off responsibilities.

Another example of a co-op is one that you actually organize yourself. If you have job-sharing options at your workplace, or if you and other parents work part-time, you could set up a baby-sitting co-op. You watch two or three other children, along with your own, on your days home; then, when you work, another parent who works a schedule different from yours watches the children. You cut down on child-care costs, know the kids are in homes with people who love them, and make sure the burden of care isn't too great on any one parent.

Possible Co-Op Parents

Parent: _____

Workdays: _____

Children (names and ages): _____

Phone: _____

Comments: _____

_____

Parent: _____

Workdays: _____

Children (names and ages): _____

Phone: _____

Comments: _____

_____

Parent: _____

Workdays: _____

Children (names and ages): _____

Phone: _____

Comments: _____

_____

Setting Up Care Nests for Sick Kids

One of the biggest challenges a working parent faces is that moment when the phone rings and the school nurse tells you your child is sick and needs to go home. Your first reaction, of course, is to want to zoom out of work as fast as you can and care for her. But what will you do tomorrow?

In larger cities, sick-child care is becoming more widely available. In these care centers, a registered nurse is on staff to care for children who are "on the mend"—no longer seriously ill or contagious.

If you don't have a facility like this in your area, or you don't feel comfortable leaving your child in sick-child care, you might want to come up with your own "care nest." Your employer, or your parent group, can approach area home day-care providers—or perhaps a grandma or two in the area—who are willing to take care of children when they aren't quite well enough to go back to school.

Careful screening is important, of course, and you should check out all references before choosing a care provider (as you would for any person responsible for the care of your child). But creating a care nest close to work enables you to check on your child during breaks and lunches and make sure she's getting quiet home care while she recuperates.

From One Parent to Another

"Maintain control of your children from the beginning, but always do it in love. Make the most of the time you have, and don't forget to say 'I love you.' Show it, too."

—Father of two who works full-time

Summary

Today's employers are becoming more aware of the family needs and responsibilities of their employees; a more well-rounded approach to benefits and flexible programs is on the horizon. If your company is not currently offering any family-supportive services—such as subsidized child care, flexible leave policies, or on-site day care—you can do things on your own to start a discussion of possibilities for the future. You can also organize a parents' group by searching out the other working parents in your department or office and coordinating child care; carpooling; or just good, old-fashioned emotional support.

In any case, knowing we're not alone in this balancing act is a comforting thought. People before us and people after us will face the same impossible schedules, the same runny noses, the same mad morning rushes to the car, and the same startled faces when we pull baby bibs from our briefcases. Parents all over the world will worry about the care their children are receiving, fret over the issue of quantity vs. quality time, pray that the educational system is doing its job, and hope that—someday, down the road—they'll know they made the right choices.

One night, as you turn out the light in your kids' room, you'll stop for a moment in the peaceful dark. By the soft glow of the night light, you'll see the kids snuggled down under the covers, the next day's clothing laid out neatly at the foot of their beds, the laundry put away, the toys shelved. In wonder, you'll walk down the stairs, which *don't* have "things to go upstairs" piled on the bottom three steps. You'll walk into the living room and see that the toys are in the toy box and there's not a trace of cat hair on the sofa. As you sit down and pick up the remote control ("You mean I actually have time to watch *television*?"), a quiet little realization washes over you: This can work.

Seem impossible right now? Don't worry—it's coming.

Notes

1. Laurie Blum, *Free Money for Day Care* (St. Louis: Fireside Books, 1992).

Back-to-Work Checklist

As you and your family prepare for your return to work, use this checklist to make sure you've covered the most important bases:

___ We have determined our family priorities.

The most important are:_____

_____

_____

_____

___ We have created a family mission statement:

_____

_____

_____

___ We have discussed the types of jobs that fit our

family's needs. They include these: _____

_____

_____

_____

_____

____ We have discussed changing responsibilities with the kids. We've explained that these things will probably change: _____

_____

_____

_____

____ We have investigated different day-care options. We considered: _____

_____

_____

_____

____ We have decided on child care and made arrangements. These are our child-care plans:

_____

_____

_____

_____

____ We have arranged back-up and emergency procedures. In case of emergency: _____

_____

_____

_____

_____

____ We have decided on and posted rules for stay-at-home children. The primary rules are these:

_____

_____

_____

_____

___ We have created and posted a sheet of emergency numbers. These are the most important numbers:

Name   Number

_____   _____

_____   _____

_____   _____

_____   _____

_____   _____

Emergency Numbers for Home and Work

Emergency Numbers for Home

Created __/__/__

Mom's work: _____

Dad's work: _____

Friend: _____

Grandma: _____

Police: _____

Fire: _____

Poison control: _____

Other: _____

Baby-sitter: _____

Preschool: _____

School: _____

After-school care: _____

In case of emergency, when Mom or Dad can't be

reached, call:_____

_____

_____

Emergency Numbers for Work

Created __/__/__

Baby-sitter: _____   Child: _____

_____   _____

Preschool: _____   Child: _____

_____   _____

School: _____   Child: _____

_____   _____

After-school care: _____   Child: _____

_____   _____

Spouse's work: _____

Friend: _____

Police: _____

Fire: _____

Poison control: _____

Other: _____

Special Instructions in Case of Emergency

Child: _____

Instruction: _____

_____

_____

Child: _____

Instruction: _____

_____

_____

Child: _____

Instruction: _____

_____

_____

Appendix

C

Family-Friendly Resources

This appendix lists sources of information on balancing home and work. You'll find basic information on general health, education, and fire prevention as well as the latest on-line offerings for parents and children.

Resources for Parents

American Academy of Pediatrics, Publications Division
141 Northwest Point Blvd.
P.O. Box 927
Elk Grove Village, IL 60009

Child Welfare League of America
440 First St. N.W., Ste. 310
Washington, DC 20001

Children's Defense Fund
25 E St. N.W.
Washington, DC 20001

Commission on Public Health
1411 K St. N.W., 12th Floor
Washington, DC 20005

Council on Family Health
420 Lexington Ave.
New York, NY 10017

La Leche League International
9616 Minneapolis Ave.
P.O. Box 1209
Franklin Park, IL 60131

National Black Child Development Institute
1463 Rhode Island Ave. N.W.
Washington, DC 20005

National Committee for Prevention of Child Abuse
332 S. Michigan Ave., Ste. 1600
Chicago, IL 60604

National Fire Protection Association
Batterymarch Park
Quincy, MA 02269

National Highway Traffic Safety Administration
400 Seventh St. S.W.
Washington, DC 20590

Associations for Children

Boy Scouts of America
1325 Walnut Hill Lane
Irving, TX 64055

Boys' Clubs of America
771 First Ave.
New York, NY 10017

Camp Fire Boys and Girls
4601 Madison Ave.
Kansas City, MO 64112

4-H
U.S. Department of Agriculture
Washington, DC 20250

Girl Scouts of the U.S.A.
420 5th Ave.
New York, NY 10018

Girls' Clubs of America
30 E. 33rd St.
New York, NY 10016

Junior Achievement
1 Education Way
Colorado Springs, CO 80906

On-Line Supports

All of the popular on-line services—America
Online, CompuServe, and Microsoft Network—
have on-line groups, called forums, specifically
related to parenting. You'll find the latest news for
parents, games for kids, and "chat rooms" where
you can discuss problems or just trade stories with
other parents across the country or around the
world.

On-line services are also good sources of
information. For example, you can access the
Internet through America Online[1] (or through
other on-line services), and get to the National
Parent Information Network, set up and supported
by the U.S. Department of Education. You'll find
all sorts of information there, including
discussions and publications on these topics:

 Assessment and testing

 Child care

 Children and the media

 Children with disabilities

 Children's health and nutrition

 Early childhood

 Gifted children

 Helping children learn at home

Older children, pre-teens, young adolescents

 Parents and families in society

 Parents and schools as partners

 Teens

This is just one example of the information available to you on-line. If you've got a computer equipped with a modem and the necessary software, give it a try.

Notes

1. From the AOL main menu, choose Internet Connection. Then select the Gopher/WAIS search and the Kids category

References

Adler, Ronald B., and Neil Towne. *Looking Out, Looking In*. 6th ed. Orlando, FL: Holt, Rinehart & Winston, 1990.

Bair, Diane, and Pamela Wright. "Coping with Five-O-Clock Frenzy." *Woman's Day*, 8 August 1995, 79.

Bernstein, Peter, and Christopher Ma. *The Practical Guide to Practically Everything*. New York: Random House, 1995.

Blum, Laurie. *Free Money for Day Care*. St. Louis: Warren H Green, Fireside Books, 1992.

Canfield, Jack, and Mark Victor Hansen. *The Aladdin Factor*. New York: Berkley Books, 1995.

Chollar, Susan. "Why Are We So Tired?" *Woman's Day*, 10 October 1995, 43.

Collingwood, Harris. "Simplicity Simplified." *Working Woman*, December 1995, 48-49.

Davis, Flora. "Psyching Out Insomnia." *Working Woman*, March 1995, 74.

"Dealing with Downshifters." *Working Woman*, December 1995, 19.

Eshleman, J. Ross. *The Family: An Introduction.* Englewood Cliffs, NJ: Paramount Publishing, Allyn & Bacon, 1974.

Farr, J. Michael. *The Very Quick Job Search.* 2nd ed. Indianapolis: JIST Works, 1996.

Grollman, Earl A., and Gerri L. Sweder. *The Working Parent Dilemma.* Boston: Beacon Press, 1983.

Henricks, Mark. "More Than Words." *Entrepreneur,* August 1995, 54-55.

Houck, Catherine. "Stress!" *Woman's Day,* 4 April 1995.

Kaye, Kenneth. *Family Rules.* New York: St. Martin's Press, 1984.

Krueger, Caryl Waller. *Working Parent—Happy Child.* Nashville, TN: Abingdon Press, 1990.

McGarvey, Robert. "Now or Never." *Entrepreneur,* October 1995.

Miller, Jeanne. *The Perfectly Safe Home.* St. Louis: Warren H Green, Fireside Books, 1991.

"The Minimal Workout." *Working Woman,* June 1995, 61.

Muscari, Ann, and Wenda Wardell Morrone. *Child Care That Works.* New York: Doubleday, 1989.

Peterson, Pipi Campbell. *Ready, Set, Organize!* Indianapolis: JIST Works, Park Avenue, 1996.

Povich, Lynn. "Get a Life." *Working Woman,* December 1995.

"Simple Child-Care Solutions." *Working Woman,* September 1995, 72.

Statistical Abstract of the United States 1995. Washington, DC: U.S. Government Printing Office, 1995.

U.S. Department of Labor. *America's Top 300 Jobs: A Complete Career Handbook*. 4th ed. Indianapolis: JIST Works, 1994.

U.S. Department of Labor. *Occupational Outlook Handbook*. 1994-1995 ed. Indianapolis: JIST Works, 1994.

Varni, James W., and Donna G. Corwin. *Time-Out for Toddlers*. New York: Berkley Books, 1991.

Working Mother Magazine, September 1995.

World Almanac 1995. Mahwah, NJ: Funk & Wagnalls, 1995.

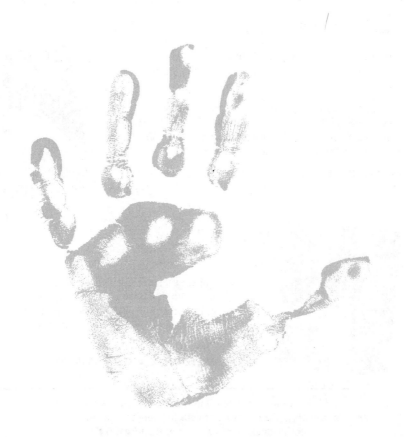

More Good Books from JIST Works, Inc., and Park Avenue Productions

America's 50 Fastest Growing Jobs, 3rd Edition
Official Information on the Best Jobs in Our Economy
J. Michael Farr, America's Career Author

Based on the latest data from the U.S. Department of Labor, this popular book contains detailed job descriptions for the 50 fastest-growing occupations and related information about each job.

ISBN 1-56370-199-5 ● Order Code J1995 ● **$14.95**

Ready, Set, Organize!
Get Your Stuff Together
Pipi Campbell Peterson

A workbook for the organizationally resistant! This book is not just about cleaning closets or organizing drawers, but about getting what we really want out of life. Entertaining with many realistic examples.

ISBN 1-57112-072-6 ● Order Code P0726 ● **$12.95**

The Resume Solution, 2nd Edition
How to Write (and Use) a Resume That Gets Results
David Swanson

This is a very, very good resume book. Just follow the step-by-step instructions to complete a *superior* resume. Painless. Easy. Effective. Includes more than 50 resume examples to help you create your own.

ISBN 1-56370-180-4 ● Order Code J1804 ● **$12.95**

Back to School
A College Guide for Adults
LaVerne L. Ludden, Ed.D.

This book addresses the concerns specific to adults returning to school. Those considering more education are guided through the decision-making process, including selecting a college oriented to adult concerns.

ISBN 1-57112-070-X ● Order Code P070X ● **$14.95**

Look for these and other fine books from JIST Works, Inc., and Park Avenue Productions at your full-service bookstore, or call us for additional information at 800-648-5478.